"If you work or volunteer for a charitable, non-profit organization, you need this book. Think of it as a consultant, staff person, and trustee. Follow Mrs. Williams' well-organized and thoughtful guidelines, and your organization will raise more money than ever before and involve your volunteers who will insist on helping again. The ultimate benefit, of course, is that you'll end up with the financial resources and volunteer support you need to accomplish your organization's important work!!!"

> — *Joseph J. Angeletti, Jr.*
> *Senior Development Officer*
> *The Yale Campaign*
> *Office of Development, School of Medicine*

"Under Warrene's leadership, we were able to increase the proceeds for our annual charity auction by 600% over the previous year."

> — *Ron Clemmer, Acquisitions Chair*
> *WNCAP Auction 93*

"The expertise Ms. Williams provided in developing a marketing strategy for advertising sales for our conference program was instrumental in making it a quality, self-funding brochure."

> — *Cynthia May, Fundraising Chair*
> *Women's Conference, 1994*

"She knows her stuff. Her book will be helpful to anyone who is undertaking a special event."

> — *Cricket Crigler, President*
> *Buncombe County Medical Auxiliary*

"User Friendly Fund$Raising is a tremendous resource for any organization planning a special event. Even experienced fundraisers will find some great tips for improving event proceeds."

> — *Andrew A. Strauss, Attorney at Law*
> *Development Comittee Chair*
> *Carolina Day School*

D1501187

USER FRIENDLY FUND$RAISING

A Step–by–Step Guide to Profitable Special Events

Warrene Williams

Published by: WorldComm® a division of Creativity, Inc.

Publisher: Ralph Roberts

Cover Design: WorldComm®

Executive Editor: Kathryn L. Hall

Editor: Carey E. Watson

Interior Design and Electronic Page Assembly: WorldComm®

Printed in the United States of America

10 9 8 7 6 5 4 3 2 1

ISBN 1–56664–065–2

Library of Congress Number: 94-60483

The author and publisher have made every effort in the preparation of this book to ensure the accuracy of the information. However, the information in this book is sold without warranty, either express or implied. Neither the author nor WorldComm will be liable for any damages caused or alleged to be caused directly, indirectly, incidentally, or consequentially by the programs or information in this book.

The opinions expressed in this book are solely those of the author and are not necessarily those of WorldComm.

WorldComm—a division of Creativity, Inc.—is a full–service publisher located at 65 Macedonia Road, Alexander, NC 28701. Phone (704) 252–9515 or Fax (704) 255–8719.

WorldComm® is distributed to the trade by Associated Publishers Group, 1501 Country Hospital Road, Nashville, TN 37218. Phone (800) 327–5113, Fax (615) 254–2450.

Much of the material printed in this book is for the use of individuals in their fundraising efforts. Reproduction in quantity is permitted only with the written permission of the author. Contact: Warrene Williams, Fund$Raisers, A Division of General Eclectic Co., 1 Lone Pine Road, Asheville, NC 28803, Phone (704)277–1677.

For the Great
G. Flo Thompson

TABLE OF CONTENTS

THE DONOR BILL OF RIGHTS

Philanthropy is based on voluntary action for the common good. It is a tradition of giving and sharing that is primary to the quality of life. To assure that philanthropy merits the respect and trust of the general public, and that donors and prospective donors can have full confidence in the not–for–profit organizations and causes they are asked to support, we declare that all donors have these rights:

I. To be informed of the organizations's mission, of the way the organization intends to use donated resources, and of its capacity to use donations effectively and for their intended purpose.

II. To be informed of the identity of those serving on the organization's governing board, and to expect the board to exercise prudent judgment in its stewardship responsibilities.

III. To have access to the organization's most recent financial statements.

IV. To be assured that their gifts will be used for the purposes for which they were given.

V. To receive appropriate acknowledgment and recognition.

VI. To be assured that information about their donations is handled with respect and with confidentiality to the extent provided by law.

VII. To expect that all relationships with individuals representing organizations of interest to the donor will be professional in nature.

VIII. To be informed whether those seeking donations are volunteers, employees of the organization or hired solicitors.

IX. To have the opportunity for their names to be deleted from mailing lists that an organization may intend to share.

X. To feel free to ask questions when making a donation and to receive prompt, truthful and forthright answers.

The American Association of Fund Raising Counsel, the Association for Healthcare Philanthropy, the Council for Advancement and Support of Education and the National Society of Fund Raising Executives have developed the above Donor's Bill of Rights.

Notes

ACKNOWLEDGEMENTS

Being the one to sit down at the word processor and write a book is not the whole story. I learned about fundraising from watching dedicated volunteers in action and from participating in the event process.

Peggy McClain, one of the best, took her fundraising seriously and although our methods were not identical, I respected her enormously. Gay Whalton initially took my thinking from the "bake sale" fundraiser to the new car raffle, and although we raised the money, there were sleepless nights before we sold enough tickets to pay for the car!

Rebecca George is proof that ability combined with sensibility in fundraising does get results and Arloa Johnson is a model for volunteerism in America.

I owe special thanks to my friends, Beverly Goldner and Terri Axford, who always set the standard for me and provide the sharing as we go about our lives.

Trisha Lester, Program Director with the North Carolina Center for NonProfits, provided timely and important information for other projects that was of value to this one as well.

Tom Rawls provided the motivation for much of my own volunteerism. His mother, Ann, is proof that service is often its own reward.

And last but not least, I'm grateful to Lynn and Whitney for their patience with me as I took a cavalier attitude toward my responsibilities to them.

Dear Reader,

It seems that if anyone should know, I should, but:

How *DO* you spell fundraising?

Webster's spells it fund–raising. One of the leading authorities on the subject uses Fund Raising or fund raising (no dash).

A publication called the Grassroots Fundraising Journal spells it "my way." The Society of Fund Raising Executives says "no dash."

The word processing software on my computer wants to put in the dash. Probably the dictionary should be the last word—after all, if everyone decided to institute their own spelling, the written word could be in chaos before too long. However, my first experience was with "fundraising" and that is the spelling that comes naturally to me and since there is plenty of precedent for it, that is the spelling I chose for this book.

All of this points out how new "fundraising" is as a field of study. Many organizations are only now beginning to treat this as a management issue as well as a "volunteer" job. The best of luck on your special event and if we can assist your organization further with its fundraising plans, please call us. It's our business.

Warrene Williams, President
Fund$Raisers
Asheville, NC
January, 1994
704–277–1677

PREFACE

GO FORWARD FUNDRAISERS

There are approximately 900,000 nonprofit organizations in the United States and many of them are competing for the donation dollars that Americans so generously give—a whopping $124.7 billion in 1992. Of that total, eighty–five to ninety percent is donated by living individuals. In order to insure that your organization shares in the money, it should implement a strategic fundraising plan. This plan is usually a combination of several different types of fundraising. Formed with input from the Board, implementation is the responsibility of the fundraising committee and the development director.

If you are a small organization with an overworked executive director and no development staff, chances are that volunteers are the driving force behind much of the fundraising. In small organizations, the board may not have established major giving programs. In that case, the majority of fundraising for your organization may come from individual donors who believe in the mission and from what is known in the business as "the special event."

Nonprofit organizations hold events for a variety of reasons. Some are not intended to raise money and may even cost money. For instance, nonprofits often hold thank–you events for their volunteers. Certainly it is possible to hold some of the events outlined in this book to simply promote "good will," but the goal ultimately is to help you and your organization plan and organize events in order to make money. In 1992, the Council for Better Business Bureaus conducted a survey that indicated that Americans already think that nonprofits spend too much money on things other than their mission (fundraising, for instance).

It is my philosophy that special events should serve very specific purposes and should not be "off the cuff." All the events held by your organization should be part of an overall plan. Here's why. Suppose you are a school K–12, or a hospital with a number of employees. If every satellite group or grade decides to do its own fundraising in addition to the plan designed by the board and the development director, the donor base begins to feel "nickel and dimed." Chances are you will have competing events going on more or less at the same time because there is no coordination. This may seem like heresy to the senior class that depends on making a few hundred dollars from a car wash to pay for prom decorations. However, it may be that the senior class could assist with the larger fundraising picture as waitstaff or ticket sellers, thus earning their prom money.

Some of the ideas discussed are probably familiar to you. It is my hope, however, that you will be able to take the ideas presented and make them fit your organization. Perhaps your organization considered an idea similar to one in this book and abandoned it for one reason or another. Maybe an event like one described is still part of your fundraising efforts. You may find that the organizational techniques and suggestions presented make it possible for you to try again with a discarded event. The aim is to increase your revenues, whether it be a new or continuing project.

If you are a nonprofit, probably needing capital for all kinds of things, consider whether it is really in the organization's best interest to go to all the time and effort of planning, organizing and executing an event without making some money. This book will help you to avoid unprofitable and "non–event" fundraisers. Nothing is more dull than standing around with

Notes

a plate of mediocre hors d'oeuvres waiting for the event to start and realizing that nothing is going to happen. Fund–raisers should have something interesting and fun going on at all times. After all, the point is to get people to return again and again, having such a good time that they actually enjoy giving you their donation dollars. This book will help you design and implement a special event that is a credit to your organization and to you. It will give you a step–by–step guide in order to minimize frustration and foul–ups.

There is no question that the planning and execution of a special event can take on the logistics of a royal wedding— without the luxury of hiring expensive caterers to do the work. My experience, gained from years of on–the–job volun- teer fundraising, has shown me that there is a need for this book. Many people (including me) starting out in fundraising have little back–up except their own intuition. This book is a how–to manual for novice fundraisers and will provide tips for the experienced as well.

Statistics about how nonprofits make money give the im- pression that there is little money in holding special events. There is. I have been involved with a variety of special event fundraisers that have been extremely successful. Many of the events described in this book were chaired by others and they have been wonderful events.

Almost every book I have read about the nonprofit sector mentions that the thing people like least about volunteering for an organization is "that they will have to ask their friends for money."

Perhaps you are that unusual person who does not mind asking for money. Still, how many times can you realistically

Notes

ask a friend or relative for money? No matter how much you believe in the mission of an organization, do you really want to ask your friends and relatives for money year after year? If I am participating in an annual giving campaign for three different organizations, can I ask my friends for a donation for each one? Of course not. However, could I send an invitation to several special events during the course of a year? Sure. Again, the individuals we are discussing have no connection to your organization—only to you.

I like to give people something back for their donation dollar; something they will enjoy so much that they will come back year after year to support the organization.

Let's take a hypothetical situation. Suppose that you are a board member of a nonprofit and that part of the commitment you must make is to ask several people for money. "Make up a list," the fundraising chair or the Board President might say. "Surely you know one or two people who can give $100 (or $500, etc.)?" Let's assume further that, yes, you do know one or two people who you think would make a donation. You make the appointment to see a friend; you feel uncomfortable—you may not want to do it but it is part of your obligation, so you ask for the money. The friend or relative is also uncomfortable, but makes the donation.

"Whew!" You think. "It's over." Unfortunately, it is not over. Why? Because next year is another year and the nonprofit will need another donation. Remember, we are not talking about giving anything back to this donor—we are speaking strictly about a donation. All this donor will get is a thank you letter. Do you think you can go back next year and ask for an even *larger* amount? Again, you may be that unusual

Notes

person who has no problem with this situation. However, if you are like me, you will be thinking of an alternative to asking this friend for further donations.

In an emergency situation, I might go *once* to someone I know and ask for a cash donation for an organization. Twice would have to be an extremely unusual situation. Three times? NO. Again, we are discussing individuals who have no connection with your organization. These are your friends and relatives. Foundations and corporations expect to give grants and donations and many employ people who deal exclusively with nonprofits. Charitable donations are ways for businesses to promote themselves within the larger community. Yes, most donations are tax deductible and that is certainly a consideration for many people. However, I am not an accountant and unless you are, be careful about giving inaccurate information regarding taxable donations. This is an area better left to the donor's or the organization's accountant.

If I am aware that a person can very easily give a donation, I am also acutely aware that I am not the only person asking. Regardless of the good reasons for asking a friend for money, it is still difficult to keep that up and maintain the friendship.

Let's review the situation. You have asked a friend or relative for money. This has created an uncomfortable situation for both of you and you have walked away with $100 (or $500). You may feel a bit resentful that the organization asked you to approach your friend or relative for a donation, even though you recognize the need and your commitment to the mission is strong. So—you have collected a one time donation.

Notes

Now, let's look at an *almost* identical situation. Your organization has decided to host a special event. For discussion purposes, we will call it a picnic on, say, Labor Day. The money raised from this picnic is necessary to further your organization's goals. However, this is the first time for this event and there will be some expenses. The nonprofit is wary of using its precious cash reserves for seed money for the event. You have decided that you need $500 to be sure you will have enough to go forward. Always keep in mind that this is fundraising—the idea is to make money for your organization, not to spend it.

You believe in the picnic and realize that without some seed money, it may not become reality. Again, you don't want to, but you go to your friend. "Your donation," you will say *(AFTER CHECKING WITH THE ORGANIZATION ACCOUNTANT),* "is deductible. Our organization hopes that you will agree to be the event's founding member. Our organization would like to name the picnic after you. You and your family will be special guests of the organization for the first picnic and you will receive the first, signed, limited edition commemorative T–shirts."

Perhaps your friend is modest. "Oh, no, don't name the event after us—that's too much. The T–shirts would be nice, though." You have come away with your donation, but you have given something in return. You feel great because you got your donation and you are off to a start on your event and your friend has a good feeling because she is getting something for her donation and helping you and your organization, too.

Now, let's go to the picnic. Your friend and her family come to the event. Your friend's name is displayed prominently

Notes

as the "founding member" on the inside cover of the program (you are probably thinking, "A program at a picnic?" More about this later in "How To Make the Most of It," Chapter V)– or on a display board at the entrance.

There are, of course, many other things going on at this picnic. For instance, a cooking contest, for which attendees must buy a vote at a cost of $1 each for their favorite cook. "Oh, look," says your friend, "there's Sally, our neighbor. She's entered the cooking contest. Oh, it's only $1. Let's buy a vote for her. Great recipe, Sally! Let's buy her 5 votes (or 10). It's for a good cause, etc." There are raffles (your friend buys $20 worth of tickets). People congratulate your friend for sponsoring such a great event. "Good job!"

There is a cash bar (not included in the ticket price) and your friend buys two beers (more about alcohol later). At the end of the picnic, there is entertainment and maybe dancing or fireworks and the food is terrific. Sally wins the cooking contest. All totaled, your friend spends $35, in addition to the seed money donation.

On the way home your friend tells her husband: "That was really great. I hope they do it again next year. It was such a success." As will be discussed in the next chapter, the organization *will* do it again next year. Your friend will attend again next year, this time paying admission of $15 ea. for adults and $7 for children (2 adults and two children). By the end of the day your friend will have spent an additional $40 on raffle tickets, drinks, games and contests. So, at the end of year two, let's total up.

Notes

Original seed money donation	$500
1st year	$ 35
2nd year, including tickets	$ 87
Total for two years	$622

These two situations began under similar circumstances: You went to a friend and asked for money. However, there are some very big differences. One is that your friend has had a good time for two years running and there is every expectation that she and her family will attend future picnics. She will tell others about it. "Oh, you should come with us to the picnic this year. We go every year. It's so much fun and it's for a good cause; the games are great, the kids love it..." and so on.

You have successfully asked for money but you do not have an awkward situation with your friend. She is very proud of the work that you do on behalf of this organization and of being a "founder." By year five, the picnic is famous in your community. Everyone has it on their calendar and it has become identified with your organization as its event. Your friend, of course, is still a "founding member," and listed on the front page of the program—or thanked from the podium, or both.

"Remember," your friend will say, "when we helped to found this picnic with $500? Now they raise tens of thousands!" It is almost a given that if your organization should need a donation from the "founders" for an emergency, your friend could be counted on to help. By now your friend is known to others in the organization. In an emergency, a

Notes

group of board members could call on her and explain the need,(remembering to thank her for her past support) and there is every reason to assume that she would be sympathetic.

In the first scenario, it is almost a given that every time you mention this organization to your friend, she is going to think, "Oh, oh. I'm going to be asked for a donation again."

The second scenario is why I like special event fundraising. You get to support your cause and the donor gets something back as well. If you provide a good enough time for your donors, they, too, will become supporters of your organization. Your friend has now become a friend of the nonprofit instead of a reluctant donor.

Notes

I.

WHAT TO DO *BEFORE* YOU DECIDE TO DO IT

One of the first things to do is to review any documentation from any previous events. If this is a first time event, there are many things to consider. To be successful, everyone involved with your fundraiser must believe in the mission of the organization which is to benefit. The biggest question before choosing any fundraiser is whether it is possible to produce. Many things may enter this. For instance, is the event you want to do legal? Some states have laws about raffles, donation drawings, charity casino events, bingo, special liquor licenses, and extra liability coverage. If you think there is a question about your proposed event, contact the organization's attorney and ask whether there are any statutes that may apply to the situation. Find out what you need to do to conform with any special requirement and then take it from there. These things are not likely to cause a problem, but they are things that should be addressed early on. Some communities may have regulations regarding certain food serving standards. These will probably be easy to comply with if you know in advance what they are.

This book addresses the person chairing the special event. However, the reader may be anyone: someone thinking of volunteering for an event, a development officer planning a fundraising strategy, or a board member. Each situation is different and the tone is for ease of writing—and reading.

Before even considering such an undertaking, it must be clear that the board and staff of the organization are supportive. You and your committee will be working with volunteers and it is difficult to fire a volunteer if things do not go well. The board and staff will certainly be attending and assisting with the actual event. They will *be there*, making introductions, thanking people for attending and helping at places like the registration table.

If you are lukewarm about the organization or if you believe that the board and staff are lukewarm about the fundraiser, you may be unable to make the commitment that will be necessary to achieve the goals for the event. Do not hesitate when asked to chair or assist if you do not have the time or the inclination. Most people will naturally turn thumbs down on an event that they do not find personally interesting and appealing. It is important that you be excited about chairing the event. Probably you have had some input about it already—and have ideas about changing or implementing it.

You are only one person. If your work schedule, family or other obligations will prevent you from carrying out a successful event, "just say no." There will be other times and there are other competent people. Do not say "yes," because you would feel guilty saying "no."

Above all, don't let yourself be emotionally blackmailed into taking on a responsibility. It will show in your work and you will have a miserable time because your heart will not be in it.

Another thing to keep in mind is that once you have made the commitment many people will depend on you. This may require more time than you had originally planned for— that is all part of it. A volunteer job is as much of a responsibility as one for which you are paid. It is much better to decline than to make up excuses later for not doing your

---

Notes

best. You may decide that you would rather serve on the committee than chair the event. There are times when I have agreed to chair an event simply because I knew that if I did not, it would not happen at all. I would have been happy to have someone come along and take the responsibility. However, I was never sorry that I agreed to chair these events. If you believe strongly in the mission of your organization, you must make a commitment of some kind. Don't be too surprised if you do not feel absolutely overjoyed to take on this big job. You may feel a mixture of excitement and resignation. Take a moment and think about the mission. If you are committed to it and you have the time to do it (or are willing to take time), a fundraiser is in the making.

Many nonprofits have a development office which directs the organization's fundraising as part of its function. As mentioned in the forward, if your organization has no formal fundraising plan, the board of trustees should begin one. There are many excellent publications (See Bibliography) which can assist the Board in this process. The special event compliments other types of types of fundraising, such as annual giving. However, unless this special event is being planned for a specific one time purpose, such as the 25th anniversary of the organization, it should be the *first of many.*

Special events take work and the first year is often the most difficult, as there are no guidelines from previous years. Do not set impossible goals for the first year. You may want to set your goal somewhat lower than you believe you will raise. In this way, the committee and the organization will not be disappointed and if you raise more, everyone will be pleased.

Notes

It takes time for an event's reputation to build in the community and each year should be more successful financially than the previous one. As a blueprint takes shape for the planning and execution of the event, there should be fewer headaches and more participation.

As you go along in the process of organizing the event, make notes. Next year's committee will appreciate it. I once chaired a fundraiser that was in its sixth year and there was not one single note from previous committees. Think of this as something valuable that is being passed from generation to generation.

If your organization is new at special event fundraising, some board and staff education may be necessary. There is probably no place within the organization for the committee to work and no place to store important documentation about the event from year to year. Continuity is a very important thing in fundraising. Although each succeeding year's events will take on a slightly different character as different individuals do the planning, the idea is to make it similar in concept. This is harder to do if there is not sufficient documentation— and documents. All the documentation needs a place to be. As of this writing, I have a case of materials for an annual fundraiser in my basement because the organization has no place for it. This is not the best system. Try to carve out a place at the organization headquarters for a "fundraising" file cabinet. As more and more things are stored on computer disk and not so much space needs to be devoted to hard copies, this should become less of a problem.

If your organization is hosting this special event for the first time, start a notebook. A spiral notebook is best. Just

Notes

tape items to notebook paper or punch holes in the items and put them in the notebook. Put every piece of paper, note, idea, receipt and form in the notebook. Take it with you wherever you go. You will constantly be making notes and writing down phone numbers of volunteers or donors. You do not want to lose these things. Even if you write "donor, phone number" on a piece of paper, you can make it neat later. After the event you can sort it out and put it in order for next year. This notebook, when complete, should contain a copy of all correspondence, every form printed for the event and each receipt for purchased items. Detailed reports from all the committees outlining procedure and suggestions for the future will eventually become part of this notebook. Additionally, it will contain your final, written report.

Think in terms of recycling. Many items that you may need for this year's event can be held over for succeeding years. Consider the purchase of items that you may need each year and buy in bulk. Printed materials that are needed for future years will be much less expensive when printed by the thousands. Make sure that there are no dates or names printed on these materials that will render them useless for future years.

Some events must have special items printed that are appropriate for only one event, so think carefully before ordering these items. I have seen events where boxes of stationery and forms with dates and names were printed unnecessarily. This is wasteful and disrespectful to the donors. For instance, if you are asking a printer for a price reduction or a donation, why ask for more than you will need? Invitations are much easier, since you will have a good idea how many you are going to send. Unless you are hosting a flower show, where

---

Notes

color might be very important, consider using inexpensive papers and one color printing.

If your organization continues an event year after year, it may be less expensive to purchase some equipment than to rent it year after year. Usually, however, my credo is: borrow it or get it donated. This way your organization does not have to worry about a secure storage area for equipment. For things like donor lists, the event notebook, forms, etc., there must be secure storage unless you are willing to keep it all until the next chair is chosen. Although you may be thinking it is impossible to lose such things, I have seen it happen again and again. If your organization has no development office, it is very important that some other place be found for storing fundraising materials.

Many special events can benefit from more than one chair-person. If a capable co-chair is available, this may make your job much easier. Even though you will have some support from the development officer or the executive director, these individuals will not be available at all times. A co-chair will give you a comrade throughout the entire special event process and you may be able to split the duties. The worst that will happen is that your co-chair will not do 50% of the work. Do not worry about it. Without the co-chair you would have done 100%.

Sometimes a board will attempt to "sell" you on a co-chair. If you do not believe you can work well with the suggested individual, discreetly let the trustee responsible for fundraising know. The co-chair must be reliable in the sense that he will not commit to something unless he intends to follow through with it. Even if he only commits to 15% of what you had hoped for, you come out ahead.

Notes

Often it is helpful to have an "honorary" chairperson. This may be a celebrity, a politician or a pillar of the community. This person is not expected to do any work on the event, except to perhaps show up for an occasional television appearance and, of course, the event. An honorary chair can sometimes open doors for acquiring donations for the event that would otherwise be closed. It is many times flattering to the person being asked and only enhances your organization's reputation to have a person of such sterling qualities as your "honorary" chair. This is a board decision and one that is important to resolve almost before the final decision of what event to hold or if to hold an event.

Before undertaking the chairmanship of a special event, you will have a few key committee people in line for certain positions. You will be spending a good deal of time with these individuals during the planning stages and it is important to have reliable people. It is not unusual that a few members of the original committee will fall by the wayside as life interferes with the project, so better too many committee members than not enough. Once again, if you are dealing with volunteers, which is often the case, there is little you can do when someone does not meet a commitment.

If you are new to a community, it is tricky to undertake the chairmanship of a major fundraiser. You may not know enough people to be able to put together a solid committee. You may be unfamiliar with the movers and shakers in the new community who can make a difference to your event. Organizations are often looking for "new blood" as established volunteers may be weary of carrying the fundraising burden. Fundraising is a good way to meet people and if you come

Notes

with a reputation for volunteerism, it will not be too long before your phone begins to ring.

Offer to be the volunteer coordinator or to do some other high profile job on the committee—explain that you appreciate the confidence that the organization must have in your ability—but say "no," unless you have access to a great group of volunteers or believe that the event requires little in the way of advance planning.

I once chaired a major fundraiser within a year of moving into a new community. It was one of the most rewarding I have ever done as I care deeply about the organization's mission. Nonetheless I would have declined had I not been approached by a tremendous committee who assured me that they would "make it happen." Approximately thirty volunteers came forward and pledged their assistance and it was a hugely successful event. The volunteer coordinator worked tirelessly on this event to recruit capable people to assist the committee chairs. At a later time, she received an award from the governor as the most outstanding volunteer in the State— and believe me, she deserved it!

Before agreeing to work on a fundraiser, meet with the Board of Trustees and find out how committed they are to the project. It is absolutely vital that you have 100% board approval and participation. After all, if you are trying to involve the larger community with this event, how can you ask others to participate if the organization's own board is not supportive? Often some education of staff is necessary before a major fundraiser. If you are charging admission, staff often feel they should attend without charge.

Notes

This fundraiser is being held to directly benefit the organization that pays the staff's salaries. Those salaries may even depend on the success of the fundraiser. Boards must educate their staffs, making clear how important it is that the organization be represented at the event. We are not talking about a high school hot–dog sale held at half–time of a basketball game. We are talking about a major fundraiser. There will sometimes be the contention from the staff that if they must be there as part of their obligation of employment, they should not have to pay. These are board questions, but their clarification is necessary before you decide to chair a fundraiser. I will not chair fundraisers where staff is not supportive. Period. Again, the public is expected to support your effort; surely the staff should, too.

Yes, committee members should pay to attend the event. This is a fundraiser—the idea is to make money. Remember, you are a volunteer who has agreed to undertake a project. Probably you will be using your own car and gasoline, your home telephone, your computer or typewriter, personal stamps, paper, etc. If you have children, it is likely that you will pay baby–sitters while you are attending meetings of all kinds. Your spouse will be taking over many family obligations during the planning stages. *You* will pay to attend the event. If you are willing to do this for your organization, paid staff and board must be supportive as well. Committee members should be encouraged to submit all receipts, however, for expenses which are incurred on behalf of the organization. If the member chooses to make a donation of certain items, that is fine, but the organization still needs to know that those expenses existed in order to have a realistic idea of what expenses it is likely to have in future years.

Notes

If this is a first time event, try to establish some type of budget for getting started. This should not be too difficult, once you have made a decision as to what type of event to hold. Naturally, you and the committee will try to get everything *donated* but if that is not possible, the board must approve the money to go forward. Once the process begins to go forward, it takes on a life of its own and it is very difficult to reverse course. One of the first things you will do is to firm up a location and after the organization has signed a contract for a certain date, there is no turning back.

If the board cannot underwrite the start–up costs, it must be decided if someone (perhaps you) can find a donor or two or three to underwrite these costs. The Board President should assist you in this if necessary. Before proceeding too far, the treasurer of the board should establish procedures for tracking the money. Often money will come in from a variety of sources. People will drop checks off at the organization; they will send them in the mail, etc. A good system must be in place for collection of proceeds. If there are 100 people selling raffle tickets, this can present a dilemma.

For a first time event, it is important that you and the board treasurer work very carefully to design a good system for collecting and tracking money. It should be clear very early on how much authority you as the chair will have to purchase necessary items. Obviously there is some point when Board approval may be necessary, but it is impossible to ask for permission for everything necessary to produce a special event. Boards who are unfamiliar with events may feel somewhat nervous about this. Explain that much time will be wasted— both yours and theirs—if you need to ask their approval for

Notes

every expenditure. Prepare an estimated budget and then get the approval of the board to proceed with periodic review. You may be able to underwrite many of the costs of the event by (a) selling advertising in the event program and (b) finding sponsors. Both of these are discussed in Chapter V.

The process for tracking money may be simple or complex depending on the event and the various ways you will incorporate raising money into the event. Will money be coming from the mail; from advertisers, from sponsors, from raffle tickets? Who will be responsible for collection and accounting? Whichever system is adopted should be agreed upon by the Board, the organization's accountant, the Executive Director, and you and your committee. Although raising money is the main point of the exercise, it is often a logistical problem. Staff may not have time or the inclination to handle transactions although it is inevitable that money will find its way to the organization offices. If money will be coming in from a variety of sources, you may need a finance committee to be on hand several hours a week at the organization offices to open mail, collect raffle ticket money, bill advertisers or whatever. If you are planning a large event, you may want to code deposits differently so as to know how much money is coming in from different sources.

This will become especially important at the event. Unless it is unusual, there will be money collected at the event. Make sure you have adequate personnel to accurately keep accounting records.

If your organization has a disorganized office system, and many nonprofits do, it may be wise to set up a special checking account. Most banks will do this for a minimum or

---

Notes

no fee. That may make it simpler to track the actual event proceeds. The accounting function is traditionally worked out by the board accountant, the executive director and the board treasurer.

With computerized, in–office accounting systems, it is simple to assign the event a number and to code each receipt and expense without a separate bank account, if staff is available to do it. Many nonprofits, struggling to perform their missions while overcoming budget deficits, are not automated. This makes it even more difficult for staff to take on the accounting function for fundraising. The committee should provide volunteers for this if that is the Board's desire. The Board's treasurer may want to take responsibility for finding cashiers for the event and for staffing the finance committee. Much consideration should be given to this process, especially with auctions.

Notes

II.

WHAT KIND OF EVENT

It may be that you have a good idea of the type of event that you would like to host. Before making a final decision, there are many things to consider.

♦ Can the event be produced annually?

♦ Are there enough committed volunteers?

♦ Is there a convenient location for the event—and would that location be available in the future for the event?

♦ Will weather be a factor?

♦ What are the projected proceeds? This may be a very difficult question for a first time event. Each year thereafter should be easier to predict, but it is advisable to have a goal in mind. If you live in a small community, you must think about attendance.

♦ Will your event conflict with other events or with school vacations, holidays, etc.? In most communities, the Chamber of Commerce keeps a calendar of events. If you have a date in mind, call them and have them put your event on their calendar. Then call the larger hotels, conference centers, theaters, etc., in your area to make sure that they do not have something scheduled of which the Chamber is not aware.

♦ Is there an organization already hosting a similar event at a different time of year? If so, will this detract from both events? If the other organization has been hosting the event for some time and it is successful, think of community relations. Will hosting a similar event cause conflict or reflect badly on your organization? If the other nonprofit has a mission that is very different, it may be that it will not matter. However, it is wise to consider very carefully before choosing to hold an event that another organization in your area may believe is "theirs."

Once you have narrowed your field of ideas, consider all of the particulars that are unique to such an event. Ideas that seem great initially may have real problems. For the sake of discussion, let's say you are thinking in terms of a benefit concert. Certainly the example is not very realistic but it is an exercise in thinking the entire event out before deciding.

Suppose you know someone who knows someone who knows Barbra Streisand and she has agreed to come for a benefit concert to your community. Of course, your initial reaction is: "Whoopi! Our problems are over." Well, they may be just beginning.

First you must find someplace to hold this event that will accommodate the thousands of people who will want to attend. Then you must think about all of the equipment and people that will come with Ms. Streisand. She may be performing free of charge, but what about her musicians and other support personnel? Will she be bringing her own equipment? Who will be responsible for setting it up and tearing it down? Will you be paying transportation for the musicians, lighting technicians, sound engineers, etc. and where will they stay?

Once you have found the auditorium, you must find out what your responsibilities are regarding its use. Will you need to clean it up? Who will take the tickets, be the ushers? Where will Ms. Streisand stay? In your guest room? Or will she require a hotel suite? Consider carefully before you accept

Notes

something on behalf of the organization (like use of a site or a benefit performance). After you have agreed to accept someone's generous contribution, it is very difficult to go back and say you cannot use it without seeming ungrateful. Be sure that a donated site for an event really meets your needs before jumping at the chance to use it just because it's free.

If you are in a large city and your organization is a theater, Ms. Streisand's offer may suit you. Your organization probably has many affluent members who would be only too happy to entertain and host the crew, etc. Your organization already has a site available to hold future benefit concerts—in fact, your board may have a list of performers who are available to assist your organization.

On the other hand, if you are a children's shelter in a small town, you may want to think about something that doesn't require such complicated logistics and potential expense.

If you believe it is appropriate, your organization may want an event oriented for adults. If you are a school, you may want to think of something that has an appeal for children. Keep in mind the limitations. Do not plan for more than you can realistically produce and do not depend on a community for more than it can provide. However, if you and your team are going to work for weeks or months to produce an event, it should be worthwhile financially.

Site selection for an event is critical. Many factors come into play. So many that I have designed a form for your use in determining whether the site is adequate for your purposes. If you forget every other thing in this book, however, I hope you will remember this:

Notes

DO NOT LEAVE THE SITE A MESS. MAKE SURE YOU HAVE ADEQUATE TIME AND CREW TO CLEAN IT UP.

This is especially true if the space is donated. The donor of the space has done enough. Unless clean–up is clearly offered in the donation, the donor will not arrange to clean up after your fundraiser.

Before you make a final decision about an event, you may want to attend one. Try to find another organization that is convenient to your community that is holding a similar event. Seeing the event unfold will be very helpful when it comes to set–up, especially for an auction. A charity auction is different from an ordinary auction.

SITE SELECTION

Address:_____

Phone Number:_____

Contact Person:_____

Cost?_____ For How Long?_____

Is adequate time allowed for set–up? _____

Is adequate time allowed for tear down?_____

Is site conveniently located?_____

Does the site lend itself to decoration—what will be required?

_____

_____

Notes

Are there restrictions for decorations?_____

_____

Is the space large enough?_____ Is the layout efficient?_____

How many people can the facility accommodate?_____

Are there adequate bathroom facilities?_____

Is there a problem with alcoholic beverages?_____

Is there convenient and adequate parking?_____

Is there: A sound system?_____ Adequate lighting?_____

Is it accessible for delivery and pick–up of items which may come from other sources (chairs, tables, chairs, glasses, etc.?

_____

Is there a kitchen or other area that can be used for catering?

_____

Is there a telephone for use in the facility?_____

Is there adequate heating or air conditioning? *This is important to consider—often you will be choosing the site during different seasons than the event.*_____

Is smoking allowed?_____ *(Does your organization even want smoking to be allowed?)*

One problem with many special event sites is that the facility may only be available for one day. This is especially true for hotel ballrooms, country club rooms, etc. One day may not be enough to decorate, set up the event and tear it down. These things must be considered before deciding on an event or a site. Do not be discouraged, however. There are

---

Notes

probably many locations which would suit your purposes that would not be open to the profit sector. Malls, school gyms or cafeterias, art galleries, or lobbies are good possibilities. Be creative: Office buildings that are closed from Friday night until Monday morning are good if they have wide corridors which could hold the right number of people. Empty buildings are terrific if you have a talented decorating crew. The owner may be able to donate the building and take a tax deduction for the donation (something that he may never have considered).

Always advise donors to check with their accountants before making assumptions about tax deductions. Laws change and you do not want to be in a position of giving tax advice. If a building is empty anyway, the owner may be more relaxed about when you can use the facility. An extra day or two for decorating, set–up and tear–down is sometimes very valuable. A big, empty space with good lighting has a lot to recommend it.

Outdoor events are, of course, different. The hazards of a continuing outdoor event are apparent. In case of bad weather, you must reschedule or have an alternate site. If you are sold on a certain type of event that must be held outside and could not be postponed or moved inside, you may want to consider a giant circus–type tent.

Do not scrap a wonderful idea until you have researched ways to go ahead with it. Tents are expensive and you may want to try to arrange for an alternate inside site and advertise well where the inside location is. Rain dates are very inconvenient. Volunteers and attendees have scheduled the event for a certain time and it may be difficult to count on them to be available twice. If you are thinking about a golf

Notes

tournament, you may be able to just go ahead with it. If you decide on an event that absolutely must be held outside, try to arrange for the site for two consecutive weekends. Advertise that if one day is rained out, it will be the following weekend.

If you live in a place with a large hotel complex or country club, you may be able to arrange to hold an outdoor event there. Such a site will have staff to help you set up and may even cater the event. Often sites that sell food do not like nonprofits to set up competitive concession stands on their grounds, so it is better to work out some kind of mutual agreement where the site provides the labor and donates part of the profits from the food concession to your organization. There are many variations on this theme. For instance, if you are holding a conference or seminar, you may be using a hotel or club. If the management likes your mission, they may allow you more opportunities for revenue using their site. It is very difficult to change a date when you are having food donated. If you have arranged for twenty restaurants to donate food on a particular day, you must hold the event on that day. This is something to consider when planning outdoor events.

The time of year is important when scheduling a special event. Unless you are counting on bringing in tourists, the summer is out: too many people, both volunteers and attendees are on vacation during the those months. Spring and fall are your best bets, as people are available and the weather is good. June is a popular month for weddings and many potential sites are booked in advance. Personally, I like early May or early November. Winter is too risky for obvious reasons

---

Notes

unless you live in Florida or California. The only exception might be a holiday event (like a Christmas house tour).

For certain types of fundraisers, especially those that have shopping integrated, consider November. Supporters may consider a November auction a Holiday shopping opportunity. If your nonprofit is a recipient of United Way funds or a similar program, be sure that your event is not conflicting with their fundraising efforts.

Let's look at some event options.

AUCTIONS

Because charity auctions are major projects that need special consideration, a good deal of planning and preparation is necessary. Charity auctions have become a big business and there are firms which specialize in putting on nonprofit auctions for a fee.

However, if your organization has enough volunteers, you can do a successful auction. Chapter III provides a blueprint for the planning and execution of an auction. However, many of the guidelines for auctions can be easily transferred to other events.

TOURNAMENTS

There are all kinds of tournaments: golf, vollcyball, bowling, tennis, etc., but the principle is the same. Your organization either charges individual or team entry fees and then awards prizes at the end. These events are easy to organize

Notes

and the sites are obvious. Get the site donated. For a golf tournament, a club or public course may donate the site for the day. Charge a set fee for each golfer—$50 or so. If you have 100 golfers, the proceeds will be $5,000. You will have some expense in trophies or cash prizes but you may be able to offset that by incorporating a raffle (having the winning golfer pull the winning ticket) or some other related "mini" events to generate more money.

Sponsorship is the "name of the game" in tournaments. Supporters of your organization will sponsor a team or an individual for the tournament. The supporters' names are printed on tournament T–shirts, on the event program and in advertising the event. X,Y,Z Co. sponsors the "Charity Team." They pay the entry fee and take a tax deduction. That leaves the team free to spend money on the other things that are going on when their team isn't playing (or after they have been eliminated).

Tournaments require few volunteers during the planning stages and several during the event. You will need people to set up nets, referee, etc., if the tournament is volleyball. Bowling and golf, of course, are different. The advantages to a tournament are that you will not need a large committee. However, unless you have access to a really great golf course and an affluent population, there is a finite amount of revenue available from a tournament. Multiply the number of teams (or individuals) by the amount you will charge for an entry fee and deduct expenses. It is very straightforward. If your organization has access to a facility for a tournament, it may want to consider doing it several times a year. Getting a site donated many times a year can be a problem. However, if

---

Notes

your organization has a site that would lend itself to a tournament of some variety, this may be an option to consider.

If your organization can find 200 bowlers to register for a tournament and each bowler pays a $10 entry fee, the proceeds will be $2,000. If you offer the winning team a prize of $300, you will have $1,700 left with very little work. Simply advertise the tournament at the bowling alley for a couple of months and get the teams to sign up by sending in a form and paying a registration fee. (Remember, the bowlers can find sponsors for their teams and the sponsor makes a charitable donation.) After giving a prize to the winning team and paying other minor expenses, does this meet the needs of your organization's fundraising goals. Events like these do not need such big commitments from volunteers year after year.

CARNIVALS AND FAIRS

Carnivals and fairs are especially good for organizations which include children in their mission. They do require considerable time and effort during the planning stages, but can be extremely profitable and worthwhile. If your organization is a school, you will have a hit event and the parents will have a good time working on it. Obviously you will need a large committee for an event like this.

Halloween is a particularly good time for a carnival. Spring is good for outside fairs, etc. For Halloween you will want to do a number of different things. As always, think in terms of a raffle in conjunction with the event. (More about this in "How to Make the Most Of It").

Notes

Let's use a school gym as a site. You will need booths: Get committee members to approach different businesses about sponsoring a booth. That way, the business builds and delivers the booth, and may even supply their employees to operate the booth. It can be the "Ameri$ Bank Fortune–Telling Booth." A bank employee dresses up as a gypsy and tells fortunes inside the booth. You can have bingo (if your State law allows) which is always profitable.

Designate one area of the school as "the haunted house." Of course you will have dart games with balloons, cotton candy, bobbing for apples, hay rides, and every other game imaginable. Each game costs a certain number of tickets. Have ticket sellers at the entrance, selling $1 tickets. That way the individual booths will not be taking money. Each booth charges "1 ticket." Have someone knowledgeable about bingo assist you with that. Try a senior citizen's complex (they may offer to run the bingo for you) or a church. Someone will know how to do it. As always, be sure that law in your State, County or City allows bingo.

Food can be either a donated buffet or concession stands with hot dogs, soft drinks, cotton candy and other carnival food. Either way you will get the food donated and volunteer labor will serve it and sell it.

Open up this event to the entire community if you can. Everyone will have a good time. Charge admission or for the food, but not both. You may do better charging for the food individually than charging a $5 admission. However, if 400 people come and spend $5 each on food and another $10 on tickets, that is $2,000 + $4,000 + whatever is raised from the raffles and bingo. More about raffles in Chapter V. If you can

---

Notes

have the Haunted House open for two or three days, you will get many children coming more than once (especially if it is really, truly HAUNTED) and you can charge as much as $2 per visit.

Again, you may try to incorporate something else into this event. Be imaginative.

THEME PARTIES

There are so many ideas for theme or special event parties that an entire book could be written (and probably has been) about just this subject. My only advice about theme parties is to be very careful not to be limiting. For instance, stay away from things like "50's parties." Anyone under 35 doesn't understand the concept. Try to make it something that has wide general appeal—and many ways to incorporate different things.

I am now going to discuss an idea for a theme party that I have never actually seen implemented. Nor have I heard of anyone implementing it. This is simply a brainstorming exercise in how special events become reality.

This idea is a "Hollywood" party. Of course, it will be held in a theater lobby. Maybe there will be a prize for the person who comes in the best costume (or does the best impersonation of a favorite movie star). Of course attendees will buy votes for their favorites (at $2 per vote). There will be a raffle, probably a trip to Hollywood and lunch with a star. Limousine service, of course and Hollywood style treatment. Raffle tickets will be $25.

Notes

There will also be an admission charge to get into the party and a silent auction of some celebrity items. The food will be, naturally, champagne and caviar. There will be ice sculptures. You get the idea. A theme party can be anything, but as mentioned in the Forward, there is nothing more dull than attending a party that is a non–event. Have something going on all the time. This party could be held, for instance, on "Oscar" night. Perhaps you could sponsor a contest for the most correct guesses about winners.

If it's the Fourth of July, try to get the President's autograph; if it's Valentine's, sponsor a "design the Valentine's Day T–shirt Design Contest or perhaps get celebrities to autograph heart candy boxes. Charge $5 to enter the contest and pay a small prize. Have the winning design made up into T–shirts and then have the winning designer sign and number the T–shirts. Auction those at the event or sell them for a high price.

Again, you get the idea. The ideas are unlimited. Since you are having a party anyway, have little side events going on to help meet fundraising goals. Your committee will have many ideas for ways to expand your event and make it more exciting.

SPORTING EVENTS

You may live in a community with two very competitive high school or college basketball (or football) teams. Perhaps these two teams would agree to play each other and donate the admission proceeds to your organization.

Notes

The publicity would guarantee a "sold out" event and if one of the schools will donate the gymnasium, there would be little in the way of expenses.

This event would, depend, naturally on your organization's mission. If young people are served by your nonprofit, this could be a very profitable fundraiser. I would only recommend this if it seems logical for your community. If you are fortunate to live in an area where professionals are training, it may be worth pursuing a charity game. Sporting events have tremendous sponsorship possibilities. However, these events require special insurance and lots of volunteers to work at the event. You may be able to get the food and drink concession proceeds donated to your organization.

Naturally, there may be other teams or types of sporting events that could be organized, depending on where you live.

MORE IDEAS

HOUSE OR GARDEN TOURS
These involve tremendous community support and chances are your community already has an organization doing house tours. If not, they are extremely popular and are worth consideration. The concept is simple.

Approach approximately ten homeowners and ask if they would allow their home to be put on "tour." Advertise for several weeks (or months) in advance and sell tickets for the "tour." Tour tickets usually sell for between $12 and $20 and it is not unusual to have several thousand people turn out in

Notes

an average size city for a house tour. Expect that you will need ten people per house as volunteers. If you cannot easily manage this, try to get another organization to help.

You must be responsible for finding people to "baby–sit" each house in order that attendees do not wander off into forbidden areas (or off with forbidden items). Having been involved with house tours as a guide, as a promoter and as an owner when my home was "on tour," I have never experienced theft or damage beyond the normal wear and tear on floors that would be expected. Most homeowners will put away small valuables and keep visitors away from storage areas. There are responsibilities that the organization must understand. If a house has wall to wall carpeting, the organization must put runners down to protect these. If it rains, this can present a problem. The owners will designate certain areas to be "off limits." Guards warn attendees away from these areas, which are normally roped off to prevent entry. It is necessary to be clear on these areas when the agreement is negotiated. Sometimes owners will not want anyone looking in the bedrooms or bathrooms. In this case the house must have enough to see without these areas that the attendees are satisfied that the house was worth the ticket price.

The great thing about house tours, as opposed to other fundraisers, is that you are guaranteed free publicity. The newspaper will print pictures of the homes and the owners—often large pictures—in color. Your chances of getting a homeowner to agree to putting a house on tour are good if they have not done it before. People are flattered that their home is a candidate for a house tour and are be glad to participate—once. Once the novelty wears off, it may be

Notes

difficult to persuade an owner to put a house "on tour." Most owners go to tremendous trouble to make sure their homes look perfect for a house tour, often buying hundreds of dollars worth of flowers, painting rooms, upgrading landscaping, etc. A friend of mine once said that he liked to put his house on tour every five years or so because it forced him to do maintenance that he would otherwise leave until the place was falling down.

Guest houses and Bed and Breakfasts often like the publicity of having their businesses on display. Usually, B&B tours take place during the early afternoon to avoid check-ins. If you live in a small town with a lively tourist business, schedule B&B and house tours during your busiest tourist week and you are guaranteed a successful fundraiser year after year. You must be able, of course, to get the B&B's to allow you to do this during their busiest times. Although this takes coordination, you will not need that many committee members to organize it. You will need volunteers during the actual tours.

If you need advice about house tours, talk to a Realtor. They have open houses all the time and are often familiar with the best houses and receptive owners. A Realtor may be your ticket to getting an owner to agree to putting a home "on tour." Also—Realtors like to help charitable organizations. You may be able to get your local Board of Realtors to provide the "housesitters/guide" service for the tour. As with most special events, your organization will want to check about extra liability insurance for house tours.

Hint: The closer the houses are together, the more easily the tour will flow. Attendees don't want to spend more time

---

Notes

driving from one house to another than touring. Also this creates a sense of excitement among the attendees if they can walk from place to place. If parking is a problem with the neighborhood, try to arrange with a bus service to shuttle attendees around. The shuttles can run in a circle from parking to house A, to house B, and along the route, dropping off and picking up attendees, and back to the parking area. That way no attendee has to wait at any house for too long before getting a ride to the next stop or back to the parking area. This is helpful, too, if houses are hard to find.

Garden tours are the same concept. If you live in an area where there are many beautiful spring flowers and there are several lovely private gardens, see if you can find a dozen or so to put on a tour.

Tickets can either be sold in advance or at each house at the time of the event. Someone at each house can either punch or sell tickets. Tickets should be pre–numbered as a way of tracking attendance and money. Assign each ticket seller certain numbers, then that person is responsible for turning in either an unsold ticket or money for a sold ticket. This system can work for any fundraiser where tickets are being sold if there is a question of tracking money. You may be able to get the cost of printing the tickets and the advertising posters for the tour underwritten by finding a sponsor whose name would be prominently displayed on the back of the ticket and on the posters.

The program should describe each house, the owners and its history—and, of course, advertising will be sold in this program. More about advertising in "How to Make the Most of It," Chapter V.

Notes

SPECIALTY AUCTIONS

Several years ago, I learned a valuable lesson from a fundraiser that took hundreds of hours of work. The concept was good, but there was a better way that I was yet to discover. Fortunately, another organization that has a mission that I like took the idea, changed it slightly and made a tremendously successful fundraiser.

The original idea was to send fabric swatches to celebrities and request that the fabric be autographed. The swatches were then sewn together into a quilt. Once the quiltmaker completed the sewing, the quilt became the prize in a raffle (also known as a donation drawing). Hundreds of celebrities received indelible ink pens, several pieces of fabric (in case they needed more than one try to get it right) and a self--addressed stamped envelope. Hundreds sent them back, too. We had so many autographs, we could have made six quilts. Autographs kept coming in for months after the winner was sleeping beneath the quilt.

The problem with this raffle was that the quilt was expensive to produce and not enough tickets were sold to make it worth the tremendous effort that went into it. There was a big expense with the postage, pens, fabric, and envelopes. The quiltmaker, thankfully, donated her services.

This idea was abandoned by my organization as the only person really happy with it was the winner of the raffle. The other organization picked up on the idea and changed it slightly. The first year they, too, sent fabric swatches to the celebrities. Each returned autograph (some elaborate) then became a pillow.

Notes

The organization held a specialty auction that auctioned each pillow. There was food and a cash bar. The first year, this auction netted in the high teens.

The next year the organization sent another item to the celebrities and asked them to sign and decorate them—and *the following year the celebrities received something else. I hesitate to go into much more detail about this specialty* auction as it is still very much ongoing and it would do a disservice to this organization to have readers all over the country leaping on their bandwagon. There are plenty of good ideas out there for organizations who would like to build on this idea. This auction raised over $40,000 in 1993—and this in a community of 25,000 people.

This nonprofit, which has a health services mission, now has "collectors" of these auction items—people who come each year and buy. If the buyer cannot be there, he previews the items and leaves a sealed bid (sometimes whatever it takes to get an item)! Auctions generate tremendous excitement and make good money, too.

SPEAKERS AND SEMINARS

If your organization is membership based and has many members that have a similar interest, consider booking a speaker or holding a seminar on a subject that would be of interest to your members (fundraising perhaps?). The speaker will charge a fee (which can be $500 per day and up) plus expenses. Your organization charges a fee for attending the seminar and keeps what is left after paying for expenses. If you can get 200 people to pay $50 for a one day seminar, that is $10,000, less expenses. Your organization will have

Notes

expenses associated with advertising the seminar, the speaker's fee and expenses, and the site. You may be able to get another organization to co–sponsor a workshop or seminar. Perhaps that is a service organization in your community that has a meeting facility that would be appropriate for your seminar, workshop or conference

If your organization has a facility where the seminar could be held, so much the better. And, if your organization does have such a facility, it can probably rent it out to other organizations for similar events. Remember, the farther away the person is, the more expense you are likely to have. If you are in California and your speaker is in New York, you may be paying for at least two nights of hotels (the night before the seminar and the night of the seminar) and a hefty plane ticket. If you can find someone close to home, he or she may be able to fly in early in the morning and out the same night.

Perhaps you can get the speaker or seminar at a reduced cost—or no cost. For instance, suppose a well-known speaker or writer endorses your organization's mission and lives close by or will be vacationing nearby. If someone is willing to ask, you may have your seminar for nothing. Again, your organization is providing a service that is important. Often people really would like to help and are flattered when asked. There is an enormous difference in asking someone for time and asking for money. I don't know why this is, but I feel it and everyone I know does. Remember that it is crucial that someone hears the speaker or reviews her material before deciding to proceed. The best thoughts do not necessarily translate to the best speaker. Make sure your choice will be well-received. Ask for an outline or overview.

Notes

CASINO FUNDRAISERS

Gambling laws vary from state to state. Usually, laws relating to charity events are different. This is an area that needs professional personnel to run the fundraiser. If your state does allow charity event gambling, there will no doubt be other organizations who have used this idea. Ask for names of reputable companies that can assist you. Raffles are usually legal, but some states have regulations which apply and you should check carefully before printing tickets and advertising posters.

MORE IDEAS ...

Other types of fundraisers include cookbooks (which can be very lucrative if marketed properly), contests of every variety (cooking, beauty, marathon races, benefit movie, theater and symphony performances, raffles, and so forth). Each organization and community has different needs. As mentioned earlier, your organization should have a strategic fundraising plan in place. The special event which you will be working on will be only a part of the overall plan.

When thinking about strategic fundraising plans, think about everything that goes on in the larger community during the year that might lend itself to a fundraising opportunity for your organization. Get the Chamber of Commerce calendar and look for any event that will draw many people: Fairs, festivals, parades, etc. All of these activities may have a fundraising opportunity for you. Your organization may be able to sponsor a "mini–event" within the larger event as a fundraiser.

These are only a few of the wonderful ideas for special events. I would love to hear from you about your ideas!

Notes

PLANNING NOTES

You are now at the point when (a) either the Board of the organization has proposed to you or (b) you are about to propose to them. Regardless of which way it goes, you and the Board should be clear about what is going to happen, when it is going to happen and how it is going to happen.

At this stage there should be no questions about staff and Board attendance at the event. If the Board is expecting you to report to them before making a final approval of the idea, you may want to prepare a written proposal. Put in as much information as you can provide with as much certainty as you are able. Outline the parameters of the proposed event.

- How many people are expected

- Proposed Admission Charge

- The Type of Event

- What Fundraising Activities will Be Going On Before and After the Event?

- Expected Proceeds

- History of the Event (Is it a New Idea? Gleaned from this book? Someone else's tried and true fundraiser? The organization's traditional event with your own personal stamp?)

Assure the Board that you will be keeping notes throughout the process and that you will be asking each committee chair to submit a written report at the end. Board members may try to pin you down as to how much money you are going to raise. Be careful not to be overly optimistic. If this is

Notes

a continuing fundraiser, you may have previous years' proceeds as goals. For a new fundraiser, it is appropriate to have expectations, but make sure they are within the realm of possibility. Committee members like working towards a goal. A giant thermometer drawn on a poster with goal marks every $500 or $1,000 has tremendous psychological impact. It is important, though, that the Board and committee not be disappointed. In other words, there is no point in making the goal $100,000 if $30,000 is a realistic expectation.

It will be necessary for you to make periodic reports to the Board as the process unfolds. Sometimes they will want you to come to a meeting, but many times a written report saves time and is sufficient. Boards have an obligation to know that things are going along as anticipated and it is necessary to keep them periodically updated. If your committee runs into a snag, ask the Board for assistance. Part of being a good Board means taking an active role sometimes.

Many small nonprofits hesitate to embark on a large special event for a variety of reasons but the main objection is usually "not enough volunteers." Do not be deterred by this. Consider the resources available through service organizations or businesses in your community. If properly educated in the mission of your organization, other groups might eagerly volunteer to provide help for your event. Before abandoning this idea, give some thought to how much your community benefits from the mission of your organization. Who specifically benefits? For instance, if you are a small domestic abuse shelter, contact a woman's organizations. Many service organizations exist to help other organizations achieve their missions. Perhaps your organization has environmental concerns as its mission. Park rangers or Eagle Scouts could

Notes

provide assistance. If your organization does not have the volunteer base itself, visit a professional association meeting and promote your idea. The association members may be excited about involving themselves with a worthwhile event.

There are many good reasons why you support the mission of the organization. Perhaps if others were educated about its purposes, they, too, would be supportive. This is what nonprofit fundraising is really about—furthering the goals of the organization and helping it to achieve its mission. The Executive Director may be happy to give a talk to a luncheon group with the idea of gaining volunteer involvement.

Notes

III.

AUCTIONS

At the back of the book, you will find a sample "Committee List" and "Calendar" for an Auction (Exhibit I), complete with descriptions. These documents will assist you in planning a committee and also provide time estimates for beginning certain segments of the project. Each fundraiser is unique and these exhibits are guidelines only.

Before plugging in a date about printing, for example, talk to several printers. At the very end of the book is a flow chart (Exhibit XII) which will also help you with the committee process. These Exhibits can be used as guidelines for other events as well. However, auctions present opportunities that many event fundraisers do not. They also require a tremendous amount of coordination and planning. Work should begin on an auction between six months and one year out, depending on how many committee members will be working and how big an event you are planning. If it is the first time your organization has sponsored an auction, one year would not be too long to start planning. You may not have your first committee meeting right away but you will start to gather ideas. One good way to do this is to find other organizations who hold auctions and ask for a copy of their most recent auction program. If you have a number of programs to study, you will glean information about interesting auction items as well as getting ideas of how other programs look. These programs will give you something to pass around at the first "all committee" meeting to get your group excited. There will be many ideas for how to get the nicest looking program for the least amount of money.

It will not help you much to know about the prices of the sample programs. Printing costs can be your biggest variable and other organizations may have traded advertising for printing or had all or part of the printing donated by a supporter or some combination. If you like a particular program and believe that a similar one would be appropriate for your event, take it around to several printers and get estimates. Attempt to recruit someone for your committee who can be helpful with printing—not necessarily someone who works for a printer but someone who *buys* considerable printing. Is there a publishing firm in your community who may use a local printer? Or perhaps a mail order catalog firm ? If the printing is done locally, someone from the catalog company may be able to assist with lower printing costs.

The same is true with the layout of the program. If you have someone on your committee who either works for or does business with a graphics design group, you may find someone to do the layout. The very best way is to find someone who has a personal computer with desktop publishing software and who is willing to do the entire layout. This will save your organization hundreds or thousands of dollars, depending on the size of the catalog and the quality of the overall product.

There may be staff available to help with clerical work. This should be clarified early on. It must be understood by all parties that this staff member will be "on the committee." You may be under time constraints and you do not want any question about work priorities.

I do not really recommend this system as staff invariably view this as work that is "extra." Most small nonprofits are stretched in staffing terms already and rarely is the staff member expected to put their regular duties aside in order to

---

Notes

complete this "extra." Consequently, what often happens is that the event work is set aside in favor of the employee's regular duties. This causes friction between the committee and the staff just at a time when everyone should be working toward the common goal of producing a quality event. Unless the Executive Director understands that the "event" staff person must be available and the staff person does not feel that these duties were "forced on him," it is much better to keep the event operation a satellite operation, keeping the Board and the Director informed but not actively involved unless the participation is voluntary.

As with most events, one of the first things to do is to select a potential site (or a few site options) and form a core committee. The core committee will usually come from the volunteer base of the organization. You may have several individuals in mind already. Ask each of the individuals you have selected if they might know someone and so on. Once that is done, call a meeting of the entire committee as it exists. Ask each person on the committee to be responsible for one portion of the event. It is preferable to have each person preassigned, at least mentally.

Ask committee members to find volunteers to serve on their committees. If they have trouble or need extra help, this is a function for the volunteer coordinator. Auctions are not inexpensive to arrange and the way to pay for your expenses is to sell program advertising. Although you will have a program advertising chair, explain to the core committee that it will be helpful if each person can bring in one or two ads in addition to what the advertising committee will sell. You may get some resistance to this idea—and there is no need to make committee members upset over it. Explain that almost

Notes

every person does business with someone on a regular basis. This can be a dry cleaner, supermarket, hairdresser, service station or appliance dealer.

Get your committee thinking: perhaps they are having some construction done in their homes—ask for an ad from the contractor. Maybe someone has recently purchased a new car or central air conditioning or hired a new landscaping or house cleaning service. Perhaps a committee member is involved with a company that uses uniforms which must be dry cleaned daily. It is unlikely that the cleaner who does this will be resistant to advertising in the event program. Almost every committee member will suddenly think of someone that they think might be receptive to the purchase of an ad. Again, some education might be necessary in this situation. Explain to the committee that events do not get produced without some expense, no matter how hard the committee works. Therefore, those costs must come from the event proceeds. Contributors like to think that their donation is going directly to support the mission of the organization, not to pay for overhead. Advertising and sponsorship are ways to underwrite the event, so that every dollar collected goes directly to fund the operations of your organization.

How much advertising do you want? I like to use this formula: one–fourth advertising and three–fourths program copy. You can charge more for the back cover, and the inside pages of the front and back covers. All of the organization's major vendors should be counted on for a large program ad. Think carefully about this. The Executive Director should provide you with a list of these vendors. For instance, if your organization has a health services mission, it may pay out

Notes

thousands of dollars yearly to physicians, pharmacies, and hospitals. If that is the case, these organizations should be asked to "advertise." This advertising can be nothing more than "Wishing X,Y,Z a Successful Event."

Use easy to remember numbers ($200 for full page, $100 for half–page and $50 for quarter–page, for instance). If you can sell the covers for $300 or even more, great. You may want to negotiate a trade with a vendor for something you need for the event, maybe a back cover of advertising for the use of the site. Remember, you are going to print this program anyway—and the more you can trade, sell or get donated to underwrite the costs, the more money you will raise for your organization. If you need to rent things like chairs and tables, try to negotiate an advertising trade with a rental agency. With adequate planning, items such as tables, etc., can usually be borrowed from a school, church or from another organization. When borrowing items like this, make sure that the name of the organization is somewhere on the item so that there is no question to whom it belongs. If they are not marked at the time they are borrowed, simply put a piece of tape on the bottom of each table or chair with the organization's initials. This tape can be removed once the items have been safely returned.

Often months must be spent collecting auction items. A central storage place must be found to keep the items. This place must be accessible, yet secure. It will be very important to have everything in one place when you begin to catalogue for the program. This can be someone's basement or an empty room at the organization's offices. For small, valuable items the organization may want to get a safe deposit box at its bank.

Notes

Auctions can be limited to certain kinds of items or they can include everything—but do keep in mind that what you are holding is an auction, not a flea market or garage sale. Presentation counts at an auction. Items must be described accurately in the program and displayed to the best possible advantage at the event. You may have as many as 500 items and the logistics of keeping track of them may seem overwhelming. It will come together at the time you begin numbering them for the catalog.

Naturally, you will need an acquisitions committee. This committee may be separated into sections, depending on the number and type of items you want to auction. For instance, if you would like to have twenty or more travel related items, you may want one group working on those alone. They will be responsible for "packaging" the trips as described below and making props for the event to display them to the best advantage. If you have arranged a trip to a specific location, get as many photographs, travel brochures and other literature as you can find. Make an attractive display which lists everything that is included in the auction item.

You will need to print gift certificates for the auction. Each item that the winning bidder cannot take home with her needs a gift certificate, signed by the donor, as proof that she is the owner of the item. Keep the gift certificates at the cashier's desk and make sure the item number is written on the certificate. Make the gift certificates a size that will easily fit into your organization's regular business envelope. Place the completed gift certificate in an envelope and write the item number on the front with a short description of the item: #23, Trip to Bahamas, is sufficient. Arrange these in numerical order and give them to the cashiers at the event. When

Notes

the winning bidder comes to pay, it will be simple to hand her the envelope, remembering to thank her, of course. It may be more efficient to split the acquisitions committee into those responsible for finding "live" auction items and those that will solicit "silent" auction items. Acquisitions can be collected geographically if your organization services a large area. In that case, split the committee up by location rather than type of item.

It is a good idea to give each committee member a list of suggested items as a guideline. Naturally, the committee will be contacting local businesses.

Large items always present transportation problems. If an item is too large or heavy to move easily but you believe it will sell, have a committee member take photographs of it, blow them up as big as possible or even take a video or slides—and auction the item this way. The winning bidder can then get a gift certificate at the auction, present it directly to the donor and collect it then. It is important for the auctioneer to mention several times when auctioning such an item that the winning bidder will be responsible for moving the item.

With an automobile, you can simply park it outside the site with a sign on it and the winning bidder can drive it away. Try to have a notary public on hand to witness the transfer of title. Of course, the donor of the car will have to be there unless it was previously signed over to the organization.

Since you will need many props, a committee member should be assigned the task of providing visual aids for auction items that cannot be viewed. Recently I participated in an auction where I was able to obtain two backstage passes to a rock concert. A poster was constructed from record album

Notes

covers, T–shirts, etc., all depicting the artist. Several people turned up just to bid on the tickets and they sold for a whopping $1,100! For an item like this, it is essential to have a visual aid and advertising. The tickets were a specialty item that had great appeal to a few people. Individuals came to that auction just to bid on the tickets. No one was more surprised than I that they brought such a price. If you have a unique item, it is important that as many people as possible know about it. If only one person had come to bid on the tickets, they might have sold for $50.

At another auction I attended recently, a donor gave a one week yachting trip along Florida's intracoastal waterway. It was essential to have large photographs of the boat, the scenery, etc. The reason I mention this is to point out the importance of working out the details of the donation. It must be clearly understood what is included. How many people can the boat accommodate? Are children allowed? Who is responsible for purchasing and preparing food? Unless the donor will be physically present at the auction to answer such questions, you can't have too much information.

Let's explore some ideas for auction items that do not require a great deal of moving or tremendous storage area.

Trips. Trips. Trips. People love to travel and if they can buy a trip for less than they would ordinarily pay and still support the organization, so much the better. There are many ways to go about getting trips, the obvious one being a donation from travel agents. Who does the asking is very important. Maybe no one on your committee knows anyone at a travel agency? Again, get members thinking. Maybe they don't do a lot of traveling personally, but maybe their wife or husband is

Notes

a member of a larger organization such as a bank or a law firm—maybe the law firm books all of its trips through a certain agent.

The more you can incorporate into the trip, the more it will sell for. For instance, suppose someone who is supportive of your organization has a second home in Florida. Get the supporter to donate the house for one week. Then—ask the donor to recommend a good restaurant in the area. Give the restaurant a call, or write them a letter. Tell them a bit about your organization's mission and then explain that you are *designing a package* spotlighting their community. In the most glowing terms, let them know that it is your understanding that they are the best in the area. Offer to *exchange* a one–quarter page ad in the auction program for four dinners.

Perhaps the supporter who donated the vacation home can get these dinners for you. Now your package includes two round–trip tickets to wherever the vacation home is, a free house for a week and the dinners. Assuming you live in a cold climate and the house is available during peak season (and your plane tickets are good for the high season), you have a package worth anywhere from $1,000–$5,000, depending on the size of the house and how many people are bidding on it. Again, get all the particulars—Are the airline tickets good anytime or do restrictions apply? Must the bidder stay over a Saturday night, for instance? Does the house have laundry facilities, a pool, it is near the beach ,or better yet, on the beach. If the house is lovely, make a display with many photos. If it is not so lovely, describe it as "quaint" or "homey" and display only a few pictures. Do not present the

---

Notes

item in a misleading way, but do make the item as attractive as possible.

At a recent auction a donor gave a house in the Bahamas for one week. The house looked thoroughly unattractive from the photographs but was directly on the beach. It was billed as a "typical Bahamian cottage." The catalog described it as a "get away from it all." It was purchased by a couple who like the water and could have cared less about luxurious accommodations.

Suppose that no one associated with your organization has a winter home in Florida that they are willing to donate. If you are able to get plane tickets to a particular location, you may be able to contact a Realtor in the community. Once again, explain the mission and what you are trying to do. This time you may want to offer a full–page ad to the Realtor in exchange for assistance in locating free lodging. This can be tried with a hotel as well. Hotels get asked frequently for donations of rooms; the offer of an *exchange* of advertising is sometimes more appealing. Another idea is to contact an organization in the "package" area which may have a mission similar to your own and explain what you are doing. Ask if they can assist you. In turn, of course, your organization will assist them in obtaining something from your area in the future.

If your auction program is large enough, airlines may be receptive to an exchange of tickets for advertising. Sponsorships are another idea. You may be able to get a travel agent to "sponsor" your auction and obtain free tickets in return for the advertising space and goodwill the agent receives by being a sponsor. Allow plenty of time for these negotiations. Many

Notes

organizations have layers of red tape to go through before getting an answer.

Large chain stores often need many weeks to give you a "yes," for a donation item. Normally you will have to write a letter to the main headquarters. Sometimes there are committees that make decisions about donations. If you are going to try to negotiate directly with an airline you will need at least six months.

Once you have your trips (or any unique items), advertise! People who would not ordinarily support your organization will show up just to bid on interesting items.

The longer you have to work on obtaining trips and the more people you can get involved, the better. At one auction, a vacation home for one week in a very special location was donated and two bidders were competing. Eventually, the bidding stopped at around $5,000. The donor then came forward and offered to give the losing bidder a week for the same amount and it was sold twice. If your committee gets an item that you believe could sell twice, it may be worthwhile to ask the donor if it can be sold more than once. An organization's office manager offered eight hours of computer training on the software of the bidder's choice—and allowed the organization to sell twenty–four hours total, so the item was sold three times.

AUTOMOBILES

Do you know someone who has a used car that they have been trying to sell without success. Perhaps they can donate the car and then take a tax deduction for the blue book value. Unless you are a CPA, ask the person to check with

Notes

their own accountant or your organization's accountant before committing. Again, don't be afraid to advertise. People will attend your auction just to bid on a car. Be sure the current owner of the car has the title handy, so there are no hold–ups.

FOOD

Try to get board members, staff members and committee members to offer their "catering services." If five staff members from your organization will cater a brunch for twenty people (they provide everything), it will sell if marketed correctly ... or a spaghetti dinner ... or Mexican night. If someone is going to throw a party anyway, this is a way to do it and help your organization at the same time. Restaurants will donate dinners, lunches, or even wine tastings, and they sell. Grocery stores will sometimes give gift baskets of gourmet food items—Try to get the items, not gift certificates.

If the items are handed to you in a grocery bag, get a committee member to arrange the items attractively in a basket, then wrap the whole thing with cellophane and put a big bow on. Presentation counts.

This same concept can be done with things like hair products, cooking utensils, art supplies, even office supplies.

OBJET D'ART

You must be careful here. Again, let it be known that this is an *auction not a flea market.* Flea markets are OK, too, but this is an auction. Art, yes. Antiques, yes. Silver and jewelry are popular. You will need to borrow a display case with a lock on it for displaying small, valuable items.

Notes

SERVICES

If a person needs a service anyway, why not buy it and support your organization, too? For instance, get a dentist to donate braces or some other dental service. Many parents of nine year olds will be bidding! Accounting services, architectural services, landscaping, haircuts, massages, manicures, handyman, wallpapering, painting, refinishing, tune–ups for cars, child care, plumbing, tree trimming. Don't turn down any service. All services sell. Individuals who have service businesses like to give several hours of free time because they hope to gain new clients. A friend of mine who does odd jobs offered me "wallpapering of one room," for an auction. He ended up wallpapering an entire small hotel.

Note of caution: Try to stay away from gift certificates for a certain amount. After all, how much can you get for a $50 gift certificate? About $50. But if the same business will give you an item, it may sell for much more. If you do accept gift certificates, you may be able to make more money by using them as "raffle" prizes. If 100 people buy a $1 raffle ticket on a $50 gift certificate, it's obvious which way is more effective.

Beware of: electronics, photo equipment, used appliances and clothing. There is no way to guarantee that machines work and clothing gives an auction a "flea market" look unless it is a fur coat or a beaded gown. You will get calls from people who want to give you things simply because they don't want to pay a service to haul them away. Ask many questions before agreeing to take an item that "needs electricity to work."

Be selective and let your committee members know in advance that you may decide not to put an item in the

---

Notes

auction if you think it looks like junk. A committee member may be hesitant to turn down an item from a friend. You must educate your committee, so that they can educate their friends. Again, if it won't bring $25 or $50 at a silent auction, you probably don't want it. Put those items aside and let someone from the organization have a garage sale later. Don't be swayed by personal taste. If you think you might be rejecting an item on this basis, ask several other people's opinion.

In an instance a few years ago, a gentleman donated an enormous, red wooden duck (I think it was a duck) from the Far East that I just hated. The donor had listed the value on the acquisitions form at $2,500. The acquisitions committee and I raised our eyebrows. Several times I took the item in and out of the catalog, undecided whether to put it in the live auction. Everyone I asked about it hated it as well. But we were all puzzled by that $2,500 value the donor placed on it. We put it in and it sold for about $3,000.

Every time I am on the fence about an item I always leave it in. When collecting items for auction from businesses don't be afraid to suggest something. Businesses are often hesitant to decide what to offer as they don't want to be seen as non–supportive but may not want to give you something that is very expensive. Pick out an item that you think is attractive but not at the top of the range of items on display. If the owner is very supportive of the organization, she may say, "Oh, I want to give you something better than that." On the other hand, if the business would have given you something less expensive than what you have picked out, most times they will give you the item you like.

Notes

Each time an item is donated, the person accepting the item on behalf of the organization must complete a three–part "acquisitions form." (See Exhibit II) One copy of the form is attached securely to the item, one copy is given to the donor as a receipt and one copy is retained by the committee for use later. These forms should be pre–numbered. The printed number is simply for ease in locating the item. You will use a different numbering system for listing items in the program.

The auctioneer can realistically auction only about fifteen to twenty items per hour. Although that may not seem like many, it is approximately one every three minutes. Therefore, if there are 300 items donated, a decision will have to be made as to which items will be "live auctioned." Typically, they will be the ones which are expected to generate the most excitement and, therefore, bring the most money.

If you have fifty high ticket items, that is a good number. These items will be listed first in the program and auctioned by a professional auctioneer in the traditional style. The remainder of the items will be sold as "silent auction," items. A "silent auction," is one where the merchandise is displayed on tables along with a piece of paper called a "bid sheet." See Exhibit III. Each person that wants to bid on an item, signs the sheet.

The first bidder will enter his or her assigned bid number on the sheet and the amount bid. Then, someone else will enter a bid number and a higher amount on the next line, and so on. The silent auction must be for a pre–specified time. (See "Auction Procedures," Exhibit VI.) Usually a warning bell is rung about ten minutes before the close of bidding,

Notes

then at the end of the bidding time, the papers are quickly collected. This method allows several hundred items to be auctioned during a pre–specified time period.

Set minimum raises on both the silent and live auction. For silent, $3 is a good raise. If the item isn't worth a $3 raise, it probably shouldn't be in the auction. The live auction will be done by a pro and you can usually be guided by that individual's instinct for minimum raises for that portion. Do try to set a value on each item, at least for the live auction and list those values in the catalog. This is easy to do; just take the donor's word for it. On the acquisitions form there will be a place for the donor to set the value. This is the amount that the donor will use to value the item for income tax purposes. The item may sell for less or for more than the stated value, but it gives bidders some idea of the value of the item (as well as the auctioneer).

It is best to try to figure up each person's silent auction total before the "Live Auction" begins. People may be unaware of how much they have spent at the silent auction portion and be hesitant to bid at the live auction until they know the total from the silent auction. This takes less time than you might think. Have a cashier for every 50–75 bid numbers. Each cashier should have a calculator. Assign Cashier I numbers 1–50, Cashier II numbers 51–100, and so on. One person can quickly look down the bid sheets and determine which number was the winning bidder and pass that sheet to the appropriate cashier. By placing them in *bid number* order all the sheets for one bid number will be together. The cashier then totals up the amount owed by each bid number and staples the sheets together.

Notes

There are a number of ways to advise attendees of the amounts. One way is to construct a large poster with all the bid numbers in a grid (see Exhibit V). The cashier then quickly writes in the amount owed next to the bid number and the attendee can check the grid. Some organizations do not like this method because it does advertise how much a certain number has spent. I don't have much problem with this because it is so simple to see who is bidding on the Live Auction items. The person will be holding up his bid card for the auctioneer to see and any interested party will know how much that person is spending. Often there is a lot of applause when an item sells for a good price after much competitive bidding. It's for a good cause and people usually don't care if others see how much they are spending.

If someone does care, there is a way around that. Simply give the person two or even three bid numbers. That way the bidder can switch cards in order to remain anonymous—or give that card to another attendee with instructions on how high to bid, etc. At one auction a couple wanted to bid on a car for their daughter as a present—and they did not want the other attendees to know they were buying it for fear someone would tell her and it was meant to be a surprise. They simply registered a separate number, gave that number to a friend with instructions and it appeared to everyone else that that person had won the car.

The best way to notify individuals about their silent auction purchases is the simplest way. Announce when the totals are finished and anyone who is interested can come to the cashier's table and find out his or her total from the silent portion. Not everyone will come to find out. Some people are not interested and some know they have spent little. It will be

Notes

those individuals who really think they may have been the winning bidder on a big ticket item or two that will be interested to know. Many people will know exactly what they have won because they stood next to the item with the intention of upping their bid right up to the last second before the bid sheets were picked up.

For the live auction you will need a clerk. The clerk will have what are called "clerking tickets," and they are available through any auction supply company (Exhibit VI). If there is an auction house in your community, they may very well give you enough to get you through several years of auctions. When the auctioneer calls out "sold," the clerk writes the winning bidder's number, the item number and the amount it sold for on a clerking ticket and a runner takes it immediately to the cashier's station. The clerk will need a small table with a good view of the auctioneer—and near enough that they can communicate if necessary. Try to set the cashiers far enough away from the auctioneer that it will not be a distraction if someone needs to settle an account and leave during the proceedings. Additionally, there must be a clear path from the clerk to the cashiers for the runners. It is extremely annoying to have the runners going back and forth through the audience, so a good deal of thought must be given to the set–up, even as early as when the site is selected. Will there be enough room to set up tables, display the silent auction items and still seat everyone for the live portion—not to mention cashier's tables, bars, food stations, and display area for the live auction items?

The cashiers must have plenty of electrical outlets for calculators and extra lighting. There must be a way for people to get their items out of the building without walking through

Notes

the audience. The silent auction items can take up a lot of room! Remember, plan for no more than one item for each two feet of display space. There must be room for attendees to stand and write their bid numbers. If the bid sheets are standard 8.5 x 11 inch sheets, mark off at least 18 inches between each sheet. Put several cups of pens and pencils on each table. Unless you are going to attach the writing utensils with string to the bid sheet, make sure you have dozens of them. Attendees will pick them up and walk around with the pen or pencil rather than returning them to the proper holder. Give committee members who will be wandering the crowd answering questions plenty of extra pens and pencils to hand out if necessary.

It is necessary during the live auction to have "spotters." These volunteers will keep an eye on the audience and alert the auctioneer to bidders. The best way to insure that the auctioneer sees the bidder is to give every bidder a "bid paddle." These are really Chinese white paddle fans with luminescent marker numbers drawn on them.

These can be made by a volunteer using wooden paint sticks for handles. Simply glue the paint stick to a piece of heavy white poster board cut into a fan shape—or any fun shape. You may be able to get pre–made white fans from a wholesale florist supplier.

If your organization needs spotters, valet parking attendants, etc., think of using local high school students or fraternity or sorority members from a college or university. If your organization has a health services mission, you may be able to get a hospital auxiliary or nurses' association to provide volunteers.

Notes

If you are serving alcoholic beverages, be sure that you do not use underage volunteers as waiters or bartenders. One reason for holding a special event on a Sunday is that you will get more volunteers who are not working at their regular professions. Since Monday is a workday, start your event early (around 5 P.M.), so that people who work can be home by 10 P.M. Five hours is plenty long for any event, even an auction.

Every auction must have a program. This program serves many functions: to thank those who sponsored, donated and worked on the event and to be a guide to the event. Also, it must list every item which is to be auctioned in numerical order. Coordinating the program is a big and critical job. The problem with an auction program is that many of the items to be auctioned will be "last minute." Do not hold up your program for these items. Every auction program has addenda pages added after the printing is completed. There is no way to avoid this. There are ways, however, to minimize the problem. From the very beginning, decide on a date after which there will be no more acceptance of auction items. This is done for reasons other than the printing deadline for the program. The committee must have time to catalog and plan the space arrangement for the event. For study purposes, a sample program layout has been added as Exhibit XI.

There must be time to catalog the items numerically and to decide which will be silent auction items and which will be live items. Descriptions must be typed for each item. This may take some time, depending on who is doing the program layout. About one week before the copy for the program needs to be at the printer is a good time to say "No more." Typically,

Notes

what will happen is that after all the copy has gone to the printer, someone will call or deliver an absolutely fantastic item which you cannot resist accepting. That is when you begin the "addendum." This page (or pages) will never go to the printer. They will be typed at the very last minute and then copied on colored paper, probably at the organization office. When the programs are collected from the printer, these addenda will be inserted (see Exhibit VII).

In addition to auction items, you will get last minute donations of props, food and other items for the event. These donors will be included in the "thank you" portion of the addendum.

The committee must have time to plan the arrangement of the items—both physically in the layout at the site and in numerical terms for the program. Approximately one week before the printer's deadline for having copy submitted, the auction chair and two or three trusted committee members must catalog every item. Many of the items will be at the central storage site—but many may be simply slips of paper with particulars.

Arrange the items from the most valuable to the least valuable using the committee copies of the "acquisitions forms." The first fifty will be the "Live Auction" items. This may be a very difficult job, because you may not be sure which items *will actually bring the most money*. Don't despair. Every auction committee agonizes over these decisions. It will not really matter. If an auction item is wanted by several competitive bidders, it will sell at the silent auction just as well.

Once you have put each acquisitions form in order from the highest to the lowest, begin to number the actual items.

Notes

You will find them by the descriptions on the acquisitions forms and because the copy that you are using is pre–numbered the same as the one that is attached to the item. The reason for not using the printed numbers on the forms is that they will not coincide with the way you want them to be numbered for display and catalog purposes. Not only should you renumber the items at this time, you should reorganize them if at all possible. That way they are all in order and when they are transported from the storage area to the auction site, it will be easier to set them up. If you have several days to set up at the event site, this is not important. On the other hand, if you are setting up the morning of the event, the more organized the items are, the easier it will be.

Imagine that it is the day of the auction. The long tables have been set up for the silent auction. They are all covered with white paper. You will go down the tables with the "bid sheets," (in numerical order, the way you want the items displayed) taping one every eighteen inches or so on the tables. Look at each bid sheet for the description of the item. If it is obvious that it will need more room than the eighteen inches, leave more space. Since each bid sheet will have a number on it, as the items begin to arrive all the person who is carrying the item into the site needs to do is find the number of the bid sheet which matches the number attached to the item. One volunteer who knows in which direction the bid sheets are going should be able to direct the items to the appropriate places.

No, it will not be this simple. Some items will be too big to put on tables. This will be discovered when the items are being catalogued at the storage facility.

Notes

"Oh, this thing is too big to put on a table!" The way to solve this problem is to put that item at the very end of the numerical sequence (even though its value may not be last) and make a note that it may need "special display."

Paintings will need easels; larger furniture pieces obviously cannot be put on tables. Since you are discovering well in advance of the event which items will need special props for display purposes, the event coordinator will have time to acquire these items.

Helpful hint: If the site has traditional window sills, you can use the sills to display paintings. This works well because it takes up no floor space at the event. There may be sites that will allow you to hang pictures on the walls, but this is rare. Try to borrow easels from art galleries, antique stores or schools if you have paintings, prints, drawings or watercolors to display. You may be able to put the banquet tables against the wall of the site and prop the paintings up—keep in mind, though, that you will only be using one side of the table for display and you may need more tables.

At the event, you will have several stations set up. One will be for registering bidders. Have each attendee who wants to bid, sign a register. Ask for a driver's license, full name, address and telephone number. The registration form should clearly state that by registering to bid, the person who accepts the bid number agrees to pay for whatever items he or she should win under that number.

If you are going to accept credit cards, get an imprint of the card and write the bid number on the imprint for the cashiers. If your organization is not set up to accept credit

Notes

cards, it is a good idea to do this for an auction. The organization's bank will set this up and it is very simple.

Many people who attend an auction will come unprepared with cash—or they may want to buy something which costs more than they have in their checking account. If they know they can "put it on a card," they may bid more.

It is very important that the cashiers have a telephone where they can call for approval of the purchase from the credit card company.

A second station should be the "direction station." Volunteers should act as guides, telling attendees where to go for food, beverages, silent auction and information about the organization. Each special event should have space set aside to educate attendees about the organization.

Some bidders may make special arrangements with the organization before the event; but it is customary for the winning bidder to pay for the item and take it with him when he leaves the event. This is another reason why I like to discourage larger items. It is very difficult for the average individual to get a grand piano home and often the costs of moving it may outweigh the advantages of buying it at auction. This is the perfect example of the item to sell via video, photograph or slide.

One of the most difficult decisions about charity auctions is what to do if someone does not pay. If the organization institutes credit card payment that will eliminate much nonpayment. Here's why. Advertise that if anyone wants to pay any part of his or her bill with a credit card, that he or she should go to the cashier's desk at the *beginning* of the evening

Notes

and register the credit card number. This allows the cashiers to get an imprint of the credit card; then each time that person's bid number comes to the cashier's desk via a runner, the cashier will call the credit card company for an authorization for that amount. Once the credit card company gives that authorization, your organization has made a sale. At the end of the night, the bidder's credit card will have been billed for the total amount of his winning bids. There is never a question.

However, if the bidder wins the item and then simply does not show up at the cashier's desk to pay and claim the item, there is little the organization can do. Yes, credit card companies do take a percentage but it does not take many "no shows" at the cashier's desk to make up for this percentage.

"No shows" are another reason why I believe in charging admission. If someone will pay $25 or $50 to attend a charity auction, there is little likelihood that he or she will bid on an item and then walk out without paying.

One of the first things organizations usually say when considering an auction is: "Where do we start?" The answer is, with a committee meeting. Gather as many people as you can get together and have a brainstorming session. After reading this book you should have a good idea about what direction you want to go.

Make up a committee list like the one in the back of the book (Exhibit I). You will not need to have many meetings of the entire committee. The chairperson, however, will spend considerable time meeting with committee chairs individually or attending their meetings.

Notes

Your event will need a professional auctioneer. Although I have never had to pay for one, I would. Don't use an amateur, unless you can find a celebrity. Attendees will be much more understanding of a celebrity. Keep in mind that the auctioneer can make a tremendous difference in the amount that an auction item will bring. They are pros and getting the most for an item is their business. One way to find a good auctioneer is, of course, to attend auctions. If you see one that you think would be effective, it won't hurt to ask for that person to donate his service.

Attending auctions will also help you to plan seating, lighting, and sound for your auction. Your auctioneer must have a portable microphone in order to "work the crowd." The site may have a sound system. Ask your auctioneer what is preferable and try to be as accommodating as possible. Also you may need a slide projector or a video screen.

In the following chapter committees will be discussed. For an auction there will be acquisitions committees in addition the other committees. An auction will require careful thought regarding set–up and logistics of moving the auction items from the storage area to the event site. The system I like is the three team system: one team at the storage site loads the items in the transportation vehicles; one team moves the items to the event site and unloads; one team places the auction items for display. The moving team then returns to the storage site and moves another group of items until all the items are moved.

The day of the event will be hectic. The more people you have, the better. The food and beverage coordinator should have a team on the site to set up food stations and bars and

Notes

should have arranged for pick–up or the delivery of food. The food/beverage team at the site should know where food, beverages, utensils, glasses, etc. should be placed.

Make sure there are plenty of trash receptacles in unobtrusive places. If not, people will be setting used plates and glasses all over the silent auction display tables. I like waitstaff to be available during the silent auction to pick up glasses, plates, etc. and to deliver drinks. This allows people to spend more time bidding and less time standing in line at the bar.

Who you will need at the Event:

The Auctioneer

The Auctioneer's Clerk

The Auctioneer's Helper: Someone to help get the audience excited and to banter back and forth with the auctioneer.

Silent Auction: One person for every five tables to assist attendees and pick up bid sheets when time is up

Cashiers: One person for every 50 bid numbers

Telephone: One person to call for credit card authorizations

Waitstaff: Coordinate with food and beverage

Runners: At least four people to assist during the live auction with displaying and moving items and running clerking tickets from the clerk to the cashiers

Spotters: Several for the live suction to assist the auctioneer (the runners can alternate with the spotters)

Bartenders: Professionals—coordinated with food and beverage

Notes

Registration Table: Two people to collect admission fees and register bidders

Extra: Clean–up; one or two people to do whatever is needed—from checking the restrooms to running out to get an item that is needed; coat check person if needed

Security

Loaders: At the end of the evening, several people to assist attendees with loading items into vehicles. If the runners are not too tired, they can serve in this capacity.

Mission Table: Every event should have a display and people available to answer questions about the organization and its goals. Staff usually take this responsibility.

It is ideal to have the auctioneer's assistant be someone who is well known and well liked in the community. This person must be fun and witty, but not so much of a ham that it takes away from the auctioneer. The Mayor is usually a good choice (unless he's running for reelection and it looks like he may lose). One look from the Mayor can often prompt a hesitant bidder into one more raise. Remember, this is all in good fun and the money will go to further the mission of your organization.

It is essential that your decorating committee has made the entire live auction "arena" into something as upscale as Sotheby's. A white tablecloth and soft lighting goes a long way in "setting the mood." Have waitresses and waiters delivering required items to the attendees—you do not want attendees missing the auction because they had to make a trip to the bar. Volunteers who are working at the event should be dressed similarly, maybe in specially designed event T–shirts. If this is

Notes

not possible, they can wear similar clothing with some distinguishing characteristic. A boutonniere can be used if there is nothing more original that presents itself. Florists will often donate these as well as flower arrangements which can be auctioned at the end of the event or given to special volunteers or donors.

One essential thing to be remembered: Every event requires borrowed items and those items must be returned after the event. This can be extremely confusing. Instruct the event coordinator to keep a log of everything that is borrowed and where it came from. He should check it in when it arrives and then make arrangements for its return. When it has been returned and this *has been confirmed by the lender, the event coordinator checks the item off list and makes a notation to write a thank–you letter to the lender.*

This is the reason for providing food donors with disposable trays. It is too easy to forget to wash and return a food tray—better to provide one and throw it away at the end than offend a lender by not returning a borrowed tray.

After the live auction ends, the entire event will erupt in chaos—this is inevitable. Everyone will want to pay, take their items and leave *first.* One way to help your attendees is to provide coffee and chocolates after the event. Some attendees will appreciate this gesture very much. This does not have to be elaborate. Paper cups and napkins will do fine. Coffee can be prepared while the auction is going on and be ready just as the auctioneer is receiving his well deserved applause.

Have someone announce that coffee and dessert are being served and often attendees will take advantage of this

---

Notes

until the lines at the cashier's counters look less lengthy. This can be assisted by valet parking, efficient coat checking and loading of the items. You may even be able to arrange a system whereby the attendee sits and sips coffee, while someone gets the car, loads the auction items in it, retrieves the coats—then brings the final credit card tally or bill for signature. This is the kind of service that will have the community talking about your event for weeks afterwards and for which attendees will promptly send in their response cards the next time!

Helpful Hint: If someone has been a major purchaser, unless there is some good reason for not doing this, have the auctioneer ask the buyer to take a bow and have a big round of applause. People like to be recognized for their good works. If someone really spends a considerable amount of money, the organization may want to do something especially nice for this donor. Something that does not cost significant money! Even a small flower arrangement with a card signed by the staff and the committee means that the organization recognizes the donor and that her support is appreciated and valued.

Notes

IV.

THE COMMITTEE

The Committee, of course, will depend upon the type of fundraiser that you have decided on, but for most event fundraisers you will need many of the following committees and perhaps more as well (refer to the committee list Exhibit I, Part 1). At the first meeting, impress on the committee chairs the importance of submitting a final report about how they went about their duties. This information will all become part of the notebook which you are keeping for future event chairpersons.

1. VOLUNTEER COORDINATOR

If you are lucky enough to have a paid staff member to serve in this capacity, wonderful. If not, a dedicated volunteer must be found to recruit other volunteers and to match them up with suitable jobs.

2. EVENT COORDINATOR

This person will make sure that the site has everything it needs in terms of lighting, sound, tables, chairs, glasses, napkins, etc. Before the event, take an inventory. Think of every possible thing that you might need down to papers, pencils, paper clips, ice cubes, etc. and think about where you are going to get them. Make a checklist. If the organization can provide certain items, write that down. If you or another committee member knows who might donate any item, write it down. Once you have firmed up the item, check it off and then make sure that the event coordinator has a plan to "get it there."

Approximately one week before the event, meet with the event coordinator to go over this list. Leave nothing to chance. "Oh, Mary is going to have Sam bring it over," is not a good answer. The event coordinator must personally talk to every person or organization who is delivering an item to the event or make arrangements for the needed item to be picked up by a volunteer. Delivery or pick–up time should be set and at the same time it must be decided how and when the item will be returned, if necessary. A sample checklist is found at the back of the book. (See Exhibit VIII)

3. FOOD AND BEVERAGE COORDINATOR

If you are having food, whether it is to be catered separately or not, this person is critical. If the event is truly a large operation, think in terms of two people: one for the bar and one for the food.

The person in charge of the food, especially if it is all to be donated, must be very organized. A person in the restaurant or catering business is preferable for this position. Chances are that such an individual will be acquainted with many of the people who will be contributing and really what is happening at your event is a catering job. If the food must be picked up from the donors, the food coordinator must have sufficient committee members to do this. Many special events are on weekends and one thing to remember about Sundays is that businesses are often closed, so plenty of advance planning may be necessary for getting the food to the event.

Make up a menu! Too often at benefits, the committee allows the restaurant or deli, etc., to decide what type of food to donate. Typically, at such an event, the menu will look

Notes

something like this: barbecued ribs, celery and carrot tray with dip, lasagna, celery and carrot tray with dip, macaroni and cheese, celery and carrot tray with dip, shish kabobs, celery and carrot tray with dip, cookies.

Avoid this. Get professional assistance to work up a menu. Unless you are having a sit–down dinner, select foods that are easy to transport, serve, eat and clean up. When the potential donor is contacted, the food and beverage coordinator can say: "This is what we are serving. What would you prefer to donate from this list?"

When the food coordinator is satisfied that there is enough of one item, simply eliminate that item from the list of choices and so on. At the end of the solicitation process you will know exactly how much of everything you have. I have used this system and it works. The food coordinator will like it, and the donors like it. The attendees will love it—no more dripping ribs on their party clothes.

If you have a good food coordinator, the menu will be a snap. You will not need more than six different items, including desserts. Each item will not be identical—as one restaurant's quiche will be different from another's. Provide disposable plastic trays for the donors to use for transporting the food. This eliminates the inevitable confusion that is caused when it is unclear which tray belongs to whom. These trays can be purchased from most party stores for about $3. If you have a volunteer willing to scout second–hand stores you may be able to buy them for as little as $0.50. If you need more than ten or fifteen, it may be worth it for someone to spend an afternoon at the Goodwill. Even the worst looking tray can be covered with foil or lettuce leaves for one night. They can then

Notes

be thrown away at the end of the event. Knowing in advance what you will be serving allows the food coordinator to plan for appropriate trays and utensils.

Additionally, with a proposed menu in place throughout the planning stages, it is easier to try to get wines and other beverages donated. If you cannot get suppliers to donate all of the wine, at the very least you will be able to get a wholesaler to select perfectly acceptable wines and other beverages that will compliment your menu at a minimum cost. Many events end up with a combination of donated and purchased beverages. It is not unusual to have many beverages left over for the next event. Plan ahead for somewhere to store these drinks.

4. PRINTED MATERIALS

If you are going to have a program for your event, you will need someone working on this almost from the beginning. For an auction, this is a must. More on program layout in Chapter 5. It is amazing the wide range of printing prices and options. Definitely shop around before choosing a printer. Getting a big printing job fully donated is difficult unless a printer is very involved with your organization. Printers do work for nonprofits all of the time and they simply cannot comp everyone's job. A program does not have to be the highest quality to look good. Shiny covers cost more—and there is a huge price difference between a booklet and something bound in a spiral binder. Printing will often be the biggest cost item and it is a rare printer who doesn't want to get paid when the printing is completed. Since you will need all of the items before you have collected the event proceeds, plan for this expense ahead.

Notes

If this fundraiser is one that requires lots of correspon-dence, it may be worthwhile for the event to have its own stationery and forms. This can be expensive, so be sure that the situation warrants it. If the committee has dozens of members, many of whom are prominent in the community, it may help you in the solicitation of items for auction or other donations, if the potential donor recognizes some of the names on the letterhead. It doesn't take too many instances to make it worthwhile to undertake some specialized printing. For some events, such as auctions, seminars, and conferences you will need printed materials that are unique to that event. All events need special advertising and invitations must have the date.

Someone within your organization or your committee may know a graphic artist who will draw your event "logo." The artist can use it as a tax deduction and you can list the artist on the inside cover of the program and/or in small print at the bottom of the letterhead as a thank–you.

I once listed the typist's name on the inside of the cover of a program as "layout supervisor." This is the kind of good will that money can't buy. The magic word in fundraising is "recognition." Thank you goes without saying. Every person who donates anything gets a thank you. Every person who purchases a ticket gets a thank you. But people love to be recognized. Do not ask a person if they want to be recognized. They will always say, "Oh, no." It has been my experience that most people love to see their name in print, so unless the person specifically asks for no publicity, give it to them!

Even if your event doesn't really need a program, it's a good idea to print one if at all possible just so you can "name names." List the committee, list the board, list the donors,

Notes

etc. Volunteers often get little recognition for their work and this is one way the organization can say thank you. The event program may be as slick as one for a Broadway show or one that is done on a committee member's word processor and printed on the organization's copy machine.

The printing process takes time but the printer selected must commit to producing the necessary documents by a certain date. A program for an auction needs to be ready a week before the event so that attendees can preview it. This is very important. Even when you think it will be ready and you have talked to the printer and explained and explained, there are times when the material is not ready when it is supposed to be. Get final copy to the printer sooner than you believe you have to. Don't hold up a program because you are waiting for copy. You will be making an addendum for last minute entries anyway.

5. ADVERTISING SALES

If you are going to print a program, you may as well sell advertising for it. This is the best way that you have to underwrite all of the costs of producing the event without cutting the actual event profit.

This is not a popular job, but after the first year it gets easier. I designed the system for advertising sales in Chapter V. Using the Williams' System, one or two people can sell between $1,000–$10,000 worth of advertising for a program. Painlessly!

Notes

6. INVITATIONS

Sending invitations to an event guarantees that you get money that you would not ordinarily collect. With the invitation you must send a response card and a return envelope. Someone must design and print both the invitation and the response cards and return response envelopes. Usually you can incorporate the invitation addressing with a general committee meeting. Have a pot–luck or something and several people can address, several others can stuff envelopes, etc. and you can do several hundred in one day. Hand addressed invitations with stamps are the best. You do not want anyone to throw away your invitation.

7. PUBLICITY

You must publicize your event and the best person to do this is a pro. Many large organizations employ people to do press releases and public relations. Try to find someone within your organization who might know such a person who is sympathetic to your cause.

Maybe your organization has a friend in the media who would serve in this capacity. The time spent locating this person will be more than saved by what such an individual can provide. Using someone who is unfamiliar with press releases, or worse yet, someone who doesn't know anyone at the newspaper, is an exercise in futility.

If your event is a big event and you can't find a pro to donate services for this job, try to negotiate a low fee to hire someone. You may need to sell a couple more program ads to pay for it. It will be worth it.

Notes

Make sure that the publicity person is completely educated about the mission of the organization and about the event. Give this person as much material as you can and encourage questions. Often publicity people are very busy and you may want to set up specific dates for progress reports or design a schedule for publicity releases. It is better if a newspaper agrees to run a certain article a bit earlier in the process than you would like—that way, if it doesn't happen, there is still time for corrective action.

If a newspaper promises to run a story about your organization during the event week, try to make sure it is early enough to do some good. Many an event chair has been disappointed to find an article about the event in the paper the day after the fact. This is actually not that unusual—that's where a pro is worth it.

It is important to decide on an advertising plan for the event and follow it as closely as possible. Advertising is costly. Obviously, the best way to get free advertising is to find a television or radio station or newspaper to co–sponsor the event. Your event may have tremendous support and even if you are unsuccessful in finding a media sponsor, the media is now aware of the event and when they are called for publicity, it will not be a "cold" call.

8. DECORATIONS
You may need several talented people to carry out the "theme" for your event. Decorations can run from the sparse to the very elaborate and decorations can cost money. Try to

Notes

get the committee to obtain items on loan (for instance, plants from a nursery) or come up with a design that does not cost a fortune.

Recently I assisted an extremely able fundraiser with an auction. She negotiated with a hospital supply company for rolls of disposable hospital sheeting to use for draping a gymnasium. It looked lovely and cost nothing. Remember, this is not a Hollywood production with an unlimited budget for set designs. One of the biggest considerations when selecting a site is the cost of decorating. You may want to take your decorations chairperson with you when viewing prospective sites.

9. EVENT SET–UP AND TEAR–DOWN

Many people will volunteer to help at the event as a way to go but not pay. I have mixed feelings about this. If you need a particular person's expertise—say, a professional bartender, I think it is understandable that the person should not be required to pay.

I prefer to have everyone except professionals pay. Obviously, an auctioneer who is donating his services doesn't pay; or the caterer. One way around this sticky problem is for the board to set aside ten tickets for "working volunteers."

The volunteers will have assigned jobs that they must carry out and it must be made very clear that the committee, in fact the entire organization has worked very hard in the planning and that it is dependent upon them to: (a) show up and (b) do the work.

If I sound skeptical about this, it is because it has been

Notes

my experience that the volunteer who doesn't want to pay is also the one who won't follow through with an assigned task. This puts the event in jeopardy, so it is very important that the volunteers selected to help at the event are absolutely dependable.

You may need other committees but each event is different and it is impossible to estimate how many people you will need. Rely on your committee members for some of the answers. Committee members themselves often know someone who will serve with them. If a committee member needs more help, this is where your volunteer coordinator can be invaluable.

The food coordinator will have a good idea how many servers, bartenders, etc. will be needed. If you follow the suggestions in Chapter V, "How to Make the Most of It," you will have a good idea about attendance in advance.

As mentioned previously, clean–up is crucial. Consider hiring a professional service to do this. The committee will be tired and so will you. Volunteers often feel that their commitment has been met once the event is officially over. If you and the owner of the facility know that a professional crew is coming in to clean after the event, it takes the pressure off during the event.

Security is also important for some events. Off duty police will sometimes donate their services, or be available at a reduced rate for nonprofit events. It is an area where it is better to be safe than sorry. If even one person in 200 has too much to drink, it is better to have security than to be forced to deal with the situation yourself. It is inexpensive and worth it.

Notes

If the event is going to be an elegant, late–night affair, you may be able to get a taxi and/or a limousine company to offer free rides home. Many attendees will appreciate this.

Obviously, a volleyball tournament in a park on Saturday afternoon may have different needs than an evening black tie event. If you are hosting a bingo game in the basement of your church for members, it is unlikely that security will be a problem.

Notes

V.

HOW TO MAKE THE MOST OF IT

Design an event that will have wide appeal. Do not believe that just because your organization itself is small that you will have limited attendance at your event. Suppose that your organization is a nursery school with less than fifty children. You may initially think that your "donor base" is limited to the parents. Not so. Your school buys snacks for the children, has telephones and buys office supplies. If your event will appeal to the children in your school, it will appeal to other children (and parents). Remember, this is an event to *benefit* the school, it does not necessarily have to be attended only by those who are involved with the school.

If you are a health services based nonprofit, you may have a larger base of support than you know. Many people are sympathetic to your cause, but don't know how to get involved. This is your opportunity to bring those people in. Remember, your organization is involved in doing good work and part of the appeal of special events is to promote public relations.

One of the best ways to make the most of your special event, as has been previously discussed, is to sell advertising in the event program. Using the Williams' System, you will have success doing this. Unfortunately, the first year the committee will have to go out and sell lots of advertising. Assign each committee member the responsibility for two or three ads. Figure how many pages your program will be and get 25% more in advertising. For discussion purposes we have been using $200 per page. A full page then sells for $200, one–half page for $100 and one–quarter page for $50.

Think about who will buy one. Your organization's law firm, accounting firm and bank. Every organization has vendors. Find out which businesses benefited most from your organization during the past year. Did you have big utility costs? Contact the utility company—and the telephone company. Some people will place ads just because they like your organization's mission—and some because they want to help the committee member.

Try to get camera ready copy, but if you are unable to, in this age of word processing, it is easy to make up an ad. Many organizations will want to run an ad that says nothing more than "A–B–C Company wishes X–Y–Z a successful benefit."

The first year it will be more difficult, but the second year will be much simpler. You will need two programs from year one. Neatly cut out each advertisement. Construct a form letter similar to the one in the back of the book (Exhibit IX). Make an advertising form (Exhibit X). Send the letter, the ad copy and the form to the advertiser along with a self–addressed envelope.

The advertiser has to do nothing more than check "yes" and send the ad copy back. If the ad does not come back in two or three weeks, the advertising committee simply gives the advertiser a friendly phone call. This will be much less time consuming than personally calling on every advertiser. Your committee should generate some new advertising each year. Using this process, each program will be easier to sell out than the previous year's.

Remind committee members, board members, staff of the organization and attendees at the event to patronize the

Notes

advertisers. If even one or two people mention that they saw the ad and that it was appreciated, the advertiser will be extremely pleased. If one of your organization's large vendors refuses to advertise in your program, point this out to the board and the executive director. There may be a more supportive vendor out there. One common refrain from banks, legal firms, insurance companies and other high end vendors is "oh, we get asked so often." Well, sure. But on the other hand, if your organization has five hundred members and they all buy insurance, isn't it worth it for the insurance company to buy a $100 ad in your program? Or, if your organization has a law firm on retainer for a few thousand dollars a year, isn't it worth it for them to give a bit of quid pro quo?

If you are going to try to get a cover ad, it may be worthwhile for the Board President to set up the appointment or call on the vendor personally. Decide in advance which vendors you will approach and what you will ask for. I ask the development officer or the Executive Director for a list of the major vendors—in descending order. If one vendor benefits substantially more from the nonprofit, I may ask the Board President to prepare the vendor for my call.

Another way to look at the situation is: Suppose you are a school. Your biggest vendor may be a book supply company—but what about a children's shoe store. Shouldn't they be supportive? You bet! Think about how the larger community benefits from your organization. You'll have an easier time in the advertising sales department.

As mentioned in Chapter IV, invitations to the event, complete with response cards are an investment worth the money and time. Here's why. Many people who support your

Notes

organization will not be able to attend for one reason or another and by sending a response card and return envelope with the invitation, you are giving these supporters a way to send money even though they cannot attend. If your board or committee thinks sending response cards is a waste of money, disagree. You will almost certainly make more money from donations sent back with response cards from people who cannot attend than it will cost you to print all of the invitations, response cards and return envelopes. And if you *don't* send response cards and return envelopes, you will not collect a dollar from all of the people on your list who are unable to attend the event. There are some events that just do not lend themselves to response cards—but if there is any way to make it work, it is worth it.

Your response card will look something like this:

YOUR ORGANIZATION NAME

Please Reserve for Saturday, November 6:

_____Benefactor Admission (s) @ $75 ea. (Includes a VIP Pass for preferred seating, complimentary hors d' oeuvres, valet parking and drinks.)

_____Patron Admission (s) @ $50 ea. (Includes a VIP pass for reserved seating, complimentary hors d' oeuvres and drinks)

_____Sponsor Admission (s) @ $25 ea. (General Admission: complimentary hors d' oeuvres and drinks.)

_____I am unable to attend the event, but I do want to help. Enclosed is my check for_____

Name (Please Print)_____

Address_____

_____

Phone:_____

*Contributions are deductible to the full extent of the law. Make checks payable to _____

No tickets will be mailed; a guest list will be at the door

You will notice that there is a small sentence at the bottom which explains that no tickets will be mailed. Tickets are a waste of time and money. There is often not enough time for the attendee to get the tickets before the event anyway. If tickets are necessary for some reason, you can have them picked up at the door. It is simple to have someone at the door to check names off a list. Attendees will know which party they are with if it is not their own name on the list.

Alphabetize the guest list and put the number in the party after the name. As people come in, make a mark after the name, i.e., Alberts, William (4).

Serving Alcohol

Alcohol presents a tricky question for some nonprofits. If you are a substance abuse clinic, it is obvious that you will not have special events that serve alcoholic beverages. Events held in church basements will probably be alcohol free, etc..

Other cases may not be as clear cut. Simply put, if your special event is being held for adults, especially if it is an evening social event, you will make more money and draw more people if you serve alcohol. This is a serious issue and should be considered carefully. Cash bars will generate extra money. If you are charging a $50 admission fee to an event, it is very hard to justify the price if the price only includes food. You will probably need a "special event" liquor license which varies from state to state. These are usually inexpensive and easy to get but something that should be checked into during the early planning stages.

Organizations with a mission which includes children or health issues often wrestle with this problem. However, if you

Notes

want to have a successful evening auction, consider very carefully before deciding not to serve alcohol. Remember, evening events may *benefit children* but they are not for children.

If your organization has been in existence for some time, it is likely that the alcohol question has been addressed and resolved. Should your nonprofit be one of the hundreds of thousands of new ones, this is a policy that should be set at the Board level. Remember, not all fundraisers are alike, so you may want to give the thumbs up to one type and down to another.

How much are you planning to charge for admission and what does the admission charge include? If you are having a sit–down dinner and wine is included, you can charge more than for appetizers, etc. I hesitate to set prices, but at the time of this writing, 1994, $50 is a good price for sit–down and $25 for "cocktails and hors d'oeuvres." In large urban areas, the admission is sometimes more, and in smaller communities, less. It is easy to find out what is reasonable in your area. If you meet with resistance, remember, if you do not charge admission, you will be losing thousands of dollars in revenue. Think about what else you will be offering: contests, silent auctions, art auctions, raffles or gambling. Casino nights are very popular, but check carefully about your state laws regarding this. Your organization will be the "house."

Raffles are as varied as events. Just about anything can be raffled, but most people like to win money or the equivalent. A friend and I designed the "Shopping Spree" raffle. It's popular, it costs nothing and its easy.

Get a committee together and assign "sections" of the business community. Try to call on as many retail businesses

---

Notes

in your community as you can and get gift certificates for any denomination, from $5 up. Some businesses will give $20, some $100 (depending on how supportive they are to your organization or you). When you have collected all of the gift certificates, total up the amount and you have a SHOPPING SPREE, WORTH $1,000, $2,000 or whatever. You may want to take two or three of the larger gift certificates and make them 2nd & 3rd prizes.

You have a raffle prize that cost nothing. Print up posters that say,

"WIN A SHOPPING SPREE WORTH $x,000"

List the names of all of the donors on the posters. This is a small thank–you for their donation. Print up raffle tickets and sell them for $5. Regardless of how much you make, you have no out of pocket cost except the printing of the posters and tickets. People love to win this prize. Try to pick the winning raffle ticket either at the event or on a local television program as part of the promotion for the event. Obviously, this raffle is not a good idea in conjunction with an auction where your committee will be asking the same businesses for items for the event.

I have been involved in raffles from everything to $10,000 in cash to new cars to turkey dinners. All of these were successful but: many restless nights are spent when the raffle proceeds must hit $10,000 or the price of the new car to become profitable. I like the shopping spree—or any other raffle that has a prize that doesn't cost anything. It takes the pressure off.

Notes

The overriding factor to consider when deciding on a raffle is: who will sell the tickets? If your organization has hundreds of members, this will not be a problem. Decide in advance how many tickets you hope to sell at how much. Deduct the cost of the prize, if there is a cost. How many tickets will each salesperson have to sell to make your goal. You will be able to tell.

Kids buy tickets too. You may want to consider a prize that will be popular with people of all ages, not just adults. A personal computer is a good option, as I found out in a recent mini–poll of children ages six to sixteen. There is sometimes hesitation on the part of adults about targeting raffles toward children and this may be a consideration. However, I sold Girl Scout Cookies door to door when I was six years old and that was fundraising at its youngest level.

Our daughter's school has a tuition raffle each year put on by the Parents' Association. It's simple: $100 for three chances or $50 for one. If you win, your child wins a year's free tuition. This raffle is almost guaranteed to have tremendous participation every year. Multiply the number of families x the $50 per ticket, less the cost of the tuition and you have your net proceeds. The wonderful thing about this raffle is that it can be done by mail. Send a flyer with a raffle entry attached and ask the parent to send a check back with the entry and retain the stub.

Another interesting fundraiser that is done at the same school: the upper school children have a "lock–in." Children from grades one through six bring their sleeping bags and $20 to the school gym at 6:00 on a Friday night. The parents pick them up at 9:00 or so the next morning. For your $20

Notes

your child gets pizza and a fun time and you get a baby–sitter for the night.

If yours is a small community, with baby–sitters at a premium, your committee may want to provide baby–sitting for parents who want to attend your event. This would be an excellent way for a class to share in the proceeds of an existing event. For parents of young children who decide at the last minute that they want to attend the event, baby––sitting is no longer a big issue. Your organization may be able to arrange this through a local nursery school. The staff might even volunteer to do this for your organization as a community service.

You will want as much free publicity for your event as you can. Board members or executive directors can go on local television to talk about the organization and the event. Try to get articles in the Sunday paper social column. Have a representative of the organization (or you) visit community service organizations like the Junior League, Junior Chamber of Commerce, Lions Club, etc. to talk about your organization.

If you have good prizes for a raffle, or great auction items, try to get photos of these in the paper. If not, pay to advertise them. Often the newspaper will give you a reduced rate for an ad. Again, this is where a public relations or media pros are invaluable.

Most of all, get the word out to your organization's supporters about the event. Generate excitement about it. Make it the place to be on that date. Get important people in the community involved. If you are having an auction, try to get city council members to act as the spotters, for instance. This will almost guarantee a newspaper article.

Notes

Maybe the mayor will offer to cook dinner for four in someone's home as an auction item. Take a picture of the mayor at the stove in her (or his) apron and take it to the newspaper. Or, get a TV station to come and film the mayor cooking and have it run at the end of the six o'clock news. It is always good to have the help of celebrities—but be forewarned. Celebrities are busy people and often they have the best intentions but for whatever reason are unable to follow through.

I have been left to muddle through half–hour television programs, plugging an event, when a celebrity was supposed to join me and didn't show at the last second. Before getting too excited about getting a celebrity to help with a fundraiser, be absolutely certain that it will really happen. At the very least, make alternate arrangements so that you are not totally dependent on that situation.

The silliest of situations can make the best fundraisers. An organization in South Carolina hosts an event called "The Ducky Derby." Attendees pay an entry fee for their numbered rubber duck to float down a river and the winner gets a great prize. This event is plugged daily on local radio and raises tens of thousands of dollars as people line up on the banks of the river to watch the rubber ducks float down.

One thing you want to know in advance is how many people will be at your fundraiser. You want to be "sold out" before the event. Here's how to do it. Before your invitations are printed, get each committee member to submit a list of ten names of people that will attend the event if invited. This should not be a problem for anyone. Do the same with the board of directors. You may have to educate everyone a bit.

Notes

You don't want names that are obviously on the organization's mailing list or that will be on three different lists. Be imaginative. This exercise should net you approximately 100 names. When you send those invitations out, you can assume that each person who attends will bring one extra person. That's 200. Now you have the committee, which may be about thirty people and the board itself and the staff and all of their significant others.

Many of the board, the staff and the committee will not send a response card. They will just show up at the door. Try to get each board member to commit to calling all of the people on their list. "Hope you got our invitation. Looking forward to seeing you."

This group is your A group. Now you will send to the organization's major donors. That is your B group. If you have enough invitations, you may want to mail to other supporters of the group. Remember, invitations and response cards cost money—no point in mailing to someone who cannot afford the admission fee. This system has worked time after time. Do not panic if one week before the event you only have 50 or 75 responses. You will have collected money from individuals who cannot attend, people will show up at the door and by the time you get staff, board, committee and volunteer workers, you will have plenty of people at your event.

Plan your event for a certain number of people. Have food for that amount. At the first committee meeting let the committee know that you hope that they will be able to "put together a table." Since the committee will have worked on the event for months, all their friends and relatives will be

---

Notes

aware of it and they will want to come to be supportive and see what it's all about. Don't worry—if you have a good event, people will show up. Unless the weather is absolutely terrible, you may be worrying about turning people away.

I was the second in command for an art auction which was being held to benefit an organization which was new to me (although the mission was not). There was much anxiety among the committee up until the last day about not enough people showing up—"oh, it will look so bare!" This event was being held in a mall atrium which was quite large.

Having been through this many times, I reassured everyone that people would come. But, in truth, even though I *had been* through it many times, I was anxious. The day of the event, I left the site at 4:30 to go home and change clothes. When I returned at 5:30 (for an event that was supposed to start at 6:00) it was standing room only. There were literally hundreds of people there (we had about 75 affirmative response cards). I could not believe it. When I asked an attendee why everyone was so early, he said, "Oh, if you wait until the time it's supposed to start, all the good food is already gone." He also informed me that it was traditional that the only time someone returned a response card was if THEY WERE NOT COMING!

If the event is well planned, adequately advertised, and if you have been thoughtful with your invitation list, you will have a good turnout. Absolutely.

For an auction, it is really helpful if you have an exciting item or two that people know will sell for a lot of money. People will come just to watch. I once saw a small auction

> **Notes**

item designed by Bette Midler sell for $3,500. It was exciting.

Sponsorships can be an important part of a fundraising event. Obviously the easiest way to get all the costs of your event underwritten is to ask someone to do it. If your organization has wide appeal and you plan the event to be well advertised and attended, there may be an opportunity to get one or two sponsors to underwrite all or part of the costs of the event—thus leaving all of the proceeds for the organization's mission. This is not a situation where the sponsor will get nothing in return for the donation.

The sponsor will get prominent mention in the event program and in all of the advertising for the event. Newspaper and television stories about the event will mention the sponsor. This is the kind of advertising that many businesses want to have. Offer a package to the potential sponsor and go with a presentation:

"Mrs. Sponsor. Our organization would like you to sponsor our first annual countywide gymnastics tournament to support the Children's Community Foundation. The tournament will have seventy competitors and we expect five thousand people to attend. Naturally, we will have expenses. Printing of a program, T–shirts for the entrants, tickets—in the amount of $5,000. We will have to pay for the site rental and decorations. Naturally, there will be special licenses and extra liability insurance premiums. If you would agree to underwrite the event costs, which would leave all the proceeds going to the mission of our organization, which is so important to our community, we would be honored to advertise your business on the back cover of the program. Your logo would be printed

---

Notes

on the T–shirts and, of course, you would be listed as a sponsor on all of the advertising which will include radio, television and newspaper." In such a situation, you will have a good chance of obtaining a corporate sponsor.

You may even want to design an event with a certain sponsor in mind. If the event goes well and the sponsor is satisfied, there is every reason to think that this is a tradition that can be carried forward year after year.

Likewise, if you are able to obtain the help of an organization in providing labor for your event the first year and it goes well, the organization is likely to do it again.

Throughout the book, celebrities have been mentioned. People like to be involved with events that have celebrity sponsorship or other items. You must start early if you want a celebrity emcee or celebrity items. It can take months to get an item back and it is really disheartening to hold an auction and then have a really good celebrity item come in the week after. Contacting a celebrity personally is often impossible and negotiations must be done through intermediaries.

One question I am often asked is how to find celebrities. In the back of any Rolling Stone magazine there will be ads for celebrity address lists. There is an excellent book which is updated regularly called *The Address Book* by Michael Levine. This book is published by Putnam and can be found or ordered from most bookstores.

Think carefully before asking for something from a celebrity. If you have a mission that you believe a celebrity supports, certainly you are more likely to get a response from that individual. Also, the simpler the request, the better your chances

Notes

of getting a response. Do not ask for money or valuables and do not waste time writing to royalty. You will get a letter back from a lady–in–waiting telling you that Princess Diana doesn't autograph T–shirts or whatever. Be sensible in your requests. Michael Jordan must get thousands of letters asking him for a used sneaker.

If you are having, say a "Mystery Ball," you may want to contact writers of mystery books for autographing. You, of course, will provide the book! I'm not saying you will get a response but if I were chairing a Halloween Carnival, I'd ask authors of horror books to autograph something.

If you are having a Country and Western Theme, send a few country singers some sheet music and ask them to auto-graph it ... or maybe send cowboy hats. Always provide the item and a convenient way for it to be returned. The fact that your organization is thoughtful in your request will make a difference.

Do not set your sights on one celebrity. You will need to ask several celebrities in order to get one response—remem-ber, it may take months for a reply, so start early. Celebrities retire, just as other people, and often retired people have extra time. I have had excellent luck with celebrities who are no longer involved in their profession on a daily basis. Many celebrities are simply so inundated with requests for items that unless their staffs know that they strongly support your organization's mission, you will not get a response. Do not be discouraged by this—if you send enough letters, you will get positive results.

Notes

One of the biggest considerations when planning an event is: will it be worth it? For instance, if you are planning an event that will take fifty people to produce and you are hoping to make $2,000—think of something else! Your volunteers will grouse about working so long and hard for such a little return. Think in terms of a monetary goal and then try to produce an event to meet those goals that will also promote goodwill for your organization. There are always ways to make a bit more if you have time and staff. So do not rule out an event immediately just based on how much you can charge for an admission fee. This holds true with celebrity items. Have a good idea about what you are going to do with them once you have them that will make it worth the effort to acquire them.

Announce at the event that you have a goal and as you get close, generate some excitement. Have the emcee or auctioneer announce that you are getting close to the goal. People will inevitably want to help to achieve that goal—after all, they are attendees and they do not want to be outdone by last year's attendees.

If your organization is a day care center, have the children do art work and auction it at the event. No matter how awful it is, people will bid on it just for fun. If you really want to make some money, get local artists to donate pieces and have an art auction.

At one auction, the idea was to pick a piece of art for use in promotional materials for the organization. The design done by an eight year old girl sold for $500, twice. How? Her dad bought it the first time, then donated it back and someone

---

Notes

else bought it the second time. Remember, it's for a good cause and if the people were not supportive, they would not be at your event.

Notes

VI.

IT'S NOT OVER UNTIL IT'S OVER

The event is over. You are celebrating that it has been so successful. Your family is letting out a collective sigh that you have all passed a milestone. Everyone is proud and you get a good night's sleep. The next day your phone rings off the wall with people calling to congratulate you on a successful event.

However, there is still work to be done. It is necessary for you to go to the site with the event coordinator to inspect the site after the clean–up and to follow up to make sure the owner of the site is satisfied. If there is a problem, it is your job to make it right. If you have followed the advice in this book and hired a professional crew, the site should be as it was before your event. If there are borrowed items which need to be returned, this must be done. I cannot stress enough the importance of this. If someone was kind enough to loan something to you or any committee member for the event, it must be returned promptly and undamaged. If something has happened to the item, everything possible must be done to compensate the owner of the item.

The committee members will submit their final reports and you will incorporate them into your own notebook. You may want to have a special get together as sort of a deadline for this to happen. As life goes on, volunteers may want to let this important aspect of the event slip.

Your own report must be put together while things are fresh in your mind and unimportant materials must be culled from the notebook and those things that are necessary must be put in order.

The media must be reminded to run photographs and a follow–up story. Perhaps you were lucky enough to have television coverage of the event.

A personal thank–you note must be written to every person who donated, volunteered for, or attended the event. It is considerate for the event chairperson to send a note to each volunteer, including committee members. In most events, one or two volunteers prove to be outstanding and either you or the organization may want to do something extra for them. Thank you's can be a big job but it is a vital part of the event process. If there is the slightest doubt about whether someone received a thank–you, send another. Nothing will hurt the next event more than a supporter who believes that he or she is unappreciated. Something printed on the office computer is not good enough. These must be hand written, hand addressed and hand stamped. This is a commitment that I get from the committee at the very beginning. The event is over— sometimes as much as one year has been spent on it and it does not matter how wonderful it was, if a donor is not properly thanked, the lack of a thank–you will be the thing remembered.

HAVE THE THANK–YOU CARDS PRINTED AT THE SAME TIME AS THE OTHER PRINTED MATERIALS; SET THE DATE OF THE FOLLOW–UP MEETING FOR ONE WEEK AFTER THE EVENT. PROVIDE SOME FOOD, DRINK AND COMPANIONSHIP AND THEN BRING OUT THE THANK–YOU'S. The committee knows that this is the last time they will probably all be together as a group and often members linger long after the last card has been stamped. Together you have accomplished something positive for your organization and those that benefit from its mission. Volunteerism has its rewards.

This meeting can be a brainstorming session as well. Each committee member will have suggestions about how things could be improved the following year—and some definitive positives will be apparent as well. All of these things should be included in someone's final report. If each committee chair submits a final report, the chair can read each report carefully and construct a report that coordinates everything and highlights certain aspects of the event. The next committee then has an organized blueprint of previous events and many mistakes will be avoided.

There may seem some additional follow–up as the accounting function catches up with the rest of the event and many times the Board likes an oral review from the event chair. Additionally, all of the material that is left from the event must be sorted, boxed and marked for next year.

Do not let the notebook go until you can personally hand it over to the next chair. If you are moving to another community, turn the notebook over to the President of the Board. The final meeting is a good place to recruit next year's chair— the event is fresh in everyone's mind and it is not too early to pass the hat. It may be difficult to get the Board to act that quickly but if it is pointed out that there is a competent and willing individual, they may see that it's never too early. Although the chair may not begin work on the event at this early time, the entire organization will know that the good work will be carried on and the committed new chair will be on the lookout for volunteers and ideas many months before actual work begins.

If you have run a successful event, there is a good possibility that you will be asked to do it again if no one else is apparent. This is a personal decision that each individual must make. In general, however, it is not a good idea for a nonprofit to become so dependent on one person for its fundraising that it is difficult for the organization to cope without that person's input. Additionally, the chair may have called in many personal favors that might not easily be repeated. It may be that you will decide to act as an advisor for the next event rather than chairing. Again, situations and communities are different.

For a first year event, sometimes the chair learns so much about fundraising and sees so many ways that the event could be improved that he will want to do it again in order to implement all that he has learned. However, a major fundraiser is involved and time consuming and for a volunteer, it may be that once is enough—at least for awhile. If your organization's mission serves society, others will carry on the work. It is important that you not believe that the organization cannot survive without you. It can and it will.

The Board will want a follow–up report once all of the receipts are in and the final reports are completed. It may be that Board members will have ideas as well that you will want to incorporate so you may have to add an addendum to your report.

It has been my experience that for weeks and sometimes months after an event there will be feedback about an event. This information can be communicated in several ways. A memo could be drafted to the Board or the next chair incorporating all of this feedback or you could simply meet with the next chair and pass the information along orally. Of course, this is dependent on whether the event is a larger, decentralized event or whether the committee is small and informal.

You may get calls from donors with tax questions. My policy is, again, to refer these calls to professionals. The donor's own accountant or the organization's accountant are the appropriate individuals in most cases.

It is a rare event that goes perfectly for everyone. Critics will be quick to point up ways to improve. Be cautious in evaluating this type of information. If the overall event is successful and the criticism is of a minor nature, which it usually is, note it but do not let isolated instances set the tone for the future. It is the larger picture that really matters. If your event has served the mission of the organization and you are secure in the knowledge that many attendees can be counted on to attend in the future, your event was a success. Congratulations!

Notes

EXHIBIT I, PART 1
COMMITTEES

ACQUISITIONS
For an auction, this committee involves everyone. A goal should be set as to the type and number of items. Live auction items should generally bring more. Smaller items can sometimes be packaged together to make one larger item. For instance, a gift certificate for a portrait setting can be put together with a hairdressing session and a "make–over." Perhaps a cooking lesson might be combined with a cookbook and a gift certificate from a kitchen store. Remember, this is an auction, not a flea market.

SPONSORSHIP
Approach corporations and other sympathetic business about becoming an "Event Sponsor." For instance, a large hospital might sponsor a fundraiser for an organization with a health services mission. If your organization has a wide membership and the event is expected to attract many people, a large retail store may have sponsorship possibilities. At your organizational meeting, discuss various potential sponsors and outline your strategy for bringing them on board.

Think about where your "clout" is.

PROGRAM ADVERTISING
Many businesses will want to be supportive of your event. Make it easy for them to advertise. Construct a simple form and use easy to remember round numbers for advertising costs. Make your program big enough that a one–eighth page ad is not 1" by 1". If you decide on a program that is 4–1/4

by 11, do not sell ads less than one–quarter page. One–eighth would be unreadable.

Obviously you cannot have a program the size of a phone book and you don't want a program that is entirely advertising. Use common sense as to how much advertising you want to sell. A good rule is : one quarter advertising—or enough money to underwrite the cost of the event.

PRINTING

This committee negotiates with printers for the best possible prices. Printing may be your biggest expense—and your biggest variable! Get many estimates and try to negotiate a trade for some advertising in your program for printing.

Make a list of all the things you will need to have printed for your event and get an estimate for the lot. What you might need:

♦ Thank–you cards
♦ Programs
♦ Advertising contracts
♦ Acquisitions forms (for auctions)
♦ Gift certificates
♦ Stationery & envelopes (a big expense—make sure it's worth it)
♦ Posters
♦ Other advertising
♦ Tickets
♦ Invitations

Notes

FOOD AND BEVERAGE

Most events incorporate food. It is advisable to get a committee member who is a member of the restaurant or catering community. If that is not possible, the person must be extremely organized as food and beverages will probably be coming from a variety of sources and these things will need to be tracked.

PROGRAM

There are many good reasons for having a program for your event. 1) It gives you a place to thank the many people who support your event and 2) You can sell advertising as a way to underwrite the cost of the event. The committee should give much consideration to the size, layout and expense of the program. Do not spend more on your program than you will get back in advertising dollars! A small program generated on someone's home computer and printed on the organization copier may have to do. Try to make it as nice as possible for the least amount of money.

One organization which traditionally printed a slick "magazine" type program decided to save money by using newsprint one year and the attendees thought the change was great ... and the organization saved about $7,000 in printing costs alone!

INVITATIONS

Should you decide to send invitations, a committee must make decisions about mailing lists. Invitations should be *hand addressed* and stamped, especially if you are charging an admission fee and sending a response card. One good way to

Notes

accomplish this is to schedule one of the "all committee" meetings and address the invitations at the same time. Fifteen people can address, stamp and stuff about 300 invitations in a short evening.

PUBLICITY

Try to recruit a professional for this job. It is almost hopeless to try to get newspaper, television or radio advertising unless you have a professional working on it—or unless you can get media sponsorship. Don't rule that out! Media sponsorships are terrific.

DECORATIONS

Decorations can be important or not, depending on the event. If they are important, chances are they are *very important.* For an auction, presentation is paramount. The person chosen for this job should have some knowledge of floral arrangements, table settings, etc. It is a good idea to take the (potential?) decorations committee chair with you on a site selection mission.

Many times decorations can be borrowed or donated. Don't rule out a good site until you've exhausted the decorations possibilities.

VOLUNTEER COORDINATOR

This key person keeps a list of all volunteers and tries to find volunteers from the community to assist when needed. A good volunteer coordinator will have many contacts with other organizations and agencies as a way of finding workers.

Notes

ARRANGEMENTS COORDINATOR

During the planning process, various things will become necessary for the production of the event, i.e., lighting, sound, tables, chairs, extension cords, glasses—whatever. This person finds those things and arranges for them to be at the event. Keeps the event checklist up to date as to what is being delivered, picked up, by whom, how it is to be returned, etc.

SET–UP AND TEAR DOWN

This committee chair works closely with Food and Beverage, Arrangements and the Volunteer Coordinator. This is a "worker" committee of people who will only be needed just before the event, during the event and immediately after the event.

CLEAN–UP

Hire a service to clean up if necessary. Do not leave this job to the committee, as everyone will be exhausted after the event and in no mood for this awful job. Have a Committee in place to supervise and make sure that borrowed items are returned, etc., but unless you are absolutely positive that you have a committed clean–up team, hire it done. Experience speaks here!

THANK YOU'S

Nothing is more important than making sure that every person who contributes to your event gets a thank you. People like to be thanked and they deserve to be. Personal, hand

Notes

written thank–you's are absolutely the best. If you really want contributors to continue to be supportive, this is the best way. A form letter with an address label just does not have the same "thank you" quality.

For different types of fundraisers, other committees will be necessary. Auctions will need people to acquire the auction items, an auctioneer, a clerk, cashiers, etc.

Show houses will need people to coordinate the designers, act as guides during the "run of the show," etc. Fund$Raisers will be happy to provide more information about specific events for seminar attendees.

ACCOUNTING

As discussed in the text, it is important that this function be worked out in advance with the Executive Director and the Board in advance.

Notes

EXHIBIT I, PART 2
PLANNING CALENDAR*

JUNE

Site Selection

Organizational Meeting

Acquisitions Committee Active

Printing Committee Active

Event Sponsor Solicitation

Printing: Limited edition prints and advertising posters must be ordered. As of this writing, the winning artwork from (*promotional event*) has been photographed and slicked for use by graphic artists in designing these items. In the past, T–shirts have been printed with the winning artwork and sold at XXX to provide capital for the auction itself. Printing of these items should be completed by July 4th if possible.

Acquisitions: This function must involve every member of the committee as we cannot have a successful auction without quality items to auction. *See suggestions on last page.*

JULY

Acquisitions Committee active

Printing Committee active

*Note: This calendar was created for an auction held in November.

AUGUST

Acquisitions Committee Active

Program Committee begins layout for program

Food & Beverage Committee Activates

Program Ad Sales

SEPTEMBER

Acquisitions Committee Active

Food & Beverage Committee Active

Publicity Committee Active

Set–up Committee Activates

First Week in September

Second All Committee Meeting

Decorations Committee organizational meeting

Invitations ordered

Publicity kick–off

Second Week in September

Set–up Committee begins tagging items

Third Week in September

First pages of program to printer

Fourth Week in September

All committees active; meetings as necessary

Notes

OCTOBER

First Week in October

Acquisitions and Set–up Committee Meeting to finalize first pages of items listings for printer

Second Week in October

Invitations Addressed and Mailed

Decorations, Set–up and Tear–down committees meet for logistics session.

Final Program to Printer

Third Week in October: 3rd Meeting of Entire Committee

Fourth Week in October: Set–up Committee begins initial work for event.

Late acquisitions compiled for addendum to program

Logistics meeting for cashiers for auction

Final all committee meeting

NOVEMBER

First Week in November

November 5: Set–up

November 6: *Event*

November 7: Tear down and clean up

Second Week in November: Thank you's and final wrap–up

Notes

EXHIBIT II
ACQUISITIONS FORM/
RECORD OF DONATION

Number (Prenumbered)

Please Print

NAME OF DONOR_____

ADDRESS OF DONOR_____PHONE_____

CITY_____STATE_____ZIP_____

DESCRIPTION OF ITEM FOR AUCTION CATALOG_____
_____
_____

GIFT'S VALUE (if known)_____

SPECIAL COMMENTS (If any, e.g., special handling or props for display, delivery instructions, etc.)
_____
_____

DONOR CONTACTED BY:

(Name)_____

(Phone)_____

Gift Certificate Required _____Yes _____No   Attached _____Yes _____No

FOR COMMITTEE USE ONLY:

ITEM #_____ PROGRAM#_____ CATEGORY_____

DONOR'S SIGNATURE: _____

*** *Three Copies Required:* White Copy—*To Acquisitions*
Yellow Copy—*Attach to Item*
Pink Copy—*Donor Retains for Tax Purposes* (Ask the organization accountant for wording pertaining to tax deductions for donors.)

EXHIBIT III
BID SHEET

ITEM NUMBER _____

Minimum Raise $3

ITEM NUMBER	BID NUMBER	NAME	AMOUNT BID
XXXXXX	XXXXXXX	XXXXX	MINIMUM BID
XXXXXX	XXXXXXX	XXXXX	***$25

***OPTIONAL MINIMUM BID

EXHIBIT IV
AUCTION
PROCEDURES

PLEASE REMEMBER TO BRING YOUR PROGRAM
TO THE AUCTION

GENERAL RULES

Each bidder must register and provide a driver's license if payment is by check. Master Card and Visa will be accepted as well as cash and checks. Each bidder will then be given a number for bidding in both the silent and live auctions.

All items are sold as is. XXXX cannot make any representations about any item, whether it be merchandise or services. Information is based on that provided by the donor.

All sales are final and there are absolutely no refunds or exchanges. Please examine the merchandise before bidding.

Payment must be made at the time of the auction unless prior arrangement is made with XXXX and no item may be removed until payment is made.

Gift certificates will be provided for all services or for items which cannot be shown.

All items must be taken from the XXX (auction site) at the conclusion of the auction or retrieved from XXXX within one week of purchase.

In the event of a dispute, the committee will make the final decision as to the winning bidder.

SILENT AUCTION AND RAFFLES

The silent auction will begin at 5:00 PM, each numbered item will have a bid sheet. If you wish to bid on an item, sign your name, enter your bid number and the amount of your bid. *Bid numbers must* be entered legibly on the bid sheet for the bid to be valid. There is a minimum raise of three dollars. At 7:00 PM a bell will sound, signalling fifteen more minutes of bidding on silent auction items. At 7:15, the bidding will close and the cashiers will total each person's bid sheets and they will be distributed before the beginning of the live auction.

Additionally, raffle tickets will be sold on certain items and tickets may be purchased for $1. Winning raffle tickets will be pulled during the break between the silent and live auctions.

LIVE AUCTION

To enter a bid, raise your bid number, signalling either the auctioneer or a spotter, who will relay auction bids.

The auctioneer and/or the committee reserves the right to refuse a bid which it deems inadequate for the item offered. When the auctioneer proclaims the item sold and announces the bid number, the item is considered to be the property of the bidder and he or she assumes responsibility for the article.

Notes

EXHIBIT V
SILENT AUCTION

Bid Number 1	Bid Number 2	Bid Number 3	Bid Number 4
Bid Number 5	Bid Number 6	Bid Number 7	

Handwritten numbers should be drawn neatly with something that can easily be seen.

EXHIBIT VI
AUCTION TICKETS

These are three part tickets; one for the Cashier, one for the Buyer and one for the organization's records. The Clerk fills out a form for each item sold. The tickets are perforated, come twelve to a sheet, and can be ordered from:

The Missouri Auction School
1600 Genessee Street
Kansas City, MO 64102
(816) 421–7117

Buyer's Name or Number:_____

Item or Lot #:_____

_____ @ $_____ = $_____

Remarks:

This receipt verifies payment and delivery of the above. Seller retains ownership until payment check is honored. Sold as is, where is. All sales final. Thank you.

Date:_____ Page #_____ Total_____

EXHIBIT VII
ADDENDUM

List here all companies, organizations, and individuals not thanked in the main portion of the program.

ADDENDUM TO THE PROGRAM

The following names have been singled out for special recognition. The Board of Directors, the Staff and the Auction Committee owe you special thanks for your contributions.

LIVE AUCTION

150 Hand carved armoire: English, circa 1790
Retail price $6,000
Donors: Hearth Interiors

SILENT AUCTION

450 Custom made quilt from the Blue Ridge Quilters/Hand made from antique fabrics
Retail Price: $3,500
Donor: Blue Ridge Quilters

---

451 One nights' stay with breakfast at Plantation House Inn
Retail Price: $200
Donor: Plantation House

---

452 Framed print, *Bahama Village*, by nationally known painter Gail Whitney
Retail Price: $750
Donor: Gail Whitney

Addenda may be placed inside the bound program at appropriate places. Devote one section to the live auction and one section for the silent auction, as laid out in the previous page. At the top or on a page by itself, make clear when the live auction begins and when the silent auction begins. Do not put too much advertising between the live auction pages, as it gets confusing for people trying to follow along. Try not to put advertising between the items.

Notes

EXHIBIT VIII
SAMPLE CHECKLISTS

Description of Checklist Item	Owner & Address if Borrowed Item	Date Borrowed	Date Returned/ Signature
Checklist Item	Action Taken	Complete	Notes

** Checklist layouts vary from event to event. I carry my notebook around at all times with extra checklist pages and if an item doesn't exactly fit the guidelines, that's OK. Write it anyway!

EXHIBIT IX
LETTER TO
ADVERTISERS

December, 19—

Dear Advertiser:

Once again, over 40 organizations are participating to present the xxxxxxx Conference to be held at the xxxxxxxxxx Inn on Saturday, xxxxxx, 1994. Enclosed is your ad copy which was printed in the 1992 Conference program.

This year's conference promises to be most exciting with a keynote speech by noted columnist xxxxxxxxx. On Saturday evening, the Conference is pleased to announce a repeat performance by the popular xxxxxxx. The program committee hopes that you will once again show your support for the xxxxxxx Conference by placing an ad in the conference program.

The program will be a high quality 81/2" by 11" booklet. Prices are listed on the enclosed form. If you would like to run the same copy, please complete the form return it to us at the address above. We will run your 1992 copy. You enclose a check or we will bill you later. Should you want to change your copy, you may simply submit that copy with the form. If you need assistance in working up new copy, please let us know and we will be glad to help.

The deadline for the program is xxxx. However, we hope to have all advertising ready to be placed in the body of the program by February 1. Your past support of the xxxxxxx

Conference is appreciated and we look forward to working with you again.

Should you have any questions or desire further information, please let me know.

Sincerely,

xxxxxxxxxxxxxxxxx

Program Advertising

Phone xxxxxxxxxxxxx

Enclosures

Notes

EXHIBIT X
ADVERTISING
CONTRACT

PLEASE SUBMIT ONLY CAMERA READY COPY

Please Check Size:

Full Page $200 (8-1/2" by 11")_____

Half Page $100_____

Quarter Page $50_____

Name of Organization:_____

Address:_____

_____

Telephone:_____

_____

Signature

_____Check Enclosed   _____Please Bill Us

Accepted by:_____

for *(Name of Organization Holding Event)*

Camera Ready Copy Enclosed:_____

NOTE: This form may be too simplified for a complex program with more than 20 or 30 ads. You may need a printed "Advertising Contract," which may involve more than one copy. For color programs, you will need more information than is provided with this form. However, simplicity works magic! If this form will work for you, *use it!*

EXHIBIT XI
AUCTION PROGRAM
PAGE OUTLINE

Cover	2. *Inside Cover* Advertising or Sponsor's Page	3. *Title Page* List the events of the evening and the times, then the menu and the title of the event.
4. *Auction Procedures Page*	5. *List* The Board of Directors of the Organization The Staff The Event Committee	6. *Thank You Page* List everyone who contributed to the event.
7. *Mission Statement* of the Organization and a letter from the Board President, Executive Director, Event Chair, etc.	8. *Listing of Auction Items* Begin listing of the auction items, interspersed with advertising.	9. *Back Cover and Inside Back Cover* This should be prime advertising space.

EXHIBIT XII
EVENT FLOW CHART

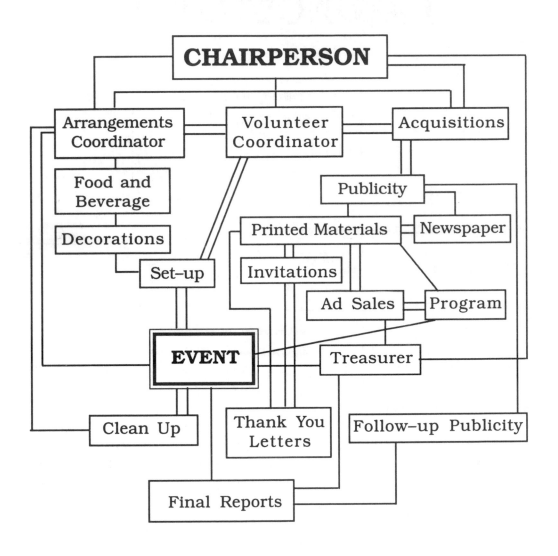

EXHIBIT XIII
ACCOUNTING FUNCTION

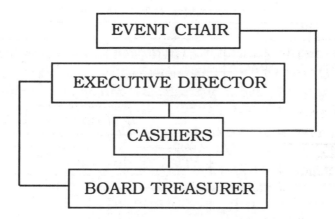

NOTE: There are a number of ways the accounting function can work. However, this flow chart works well. The Event Chair charts the sales before the event and then turns the receipts over to the Executive Director, who, in turn keeps the Treasurer informed. At the event, the Board Treasurer accepts responsibility for the cashiering function with volunteers *chosen by the Treasurer*. There may be a bookkeeper at the organization offices who will placed in charge of tracking recipts. However, this system must be set up well in advance.

Bibliography

Barry, Bryan, W. *Strategic Planning Workbook for Nonprofit Organizations.* St. Paul, MN: Amherst H. Wilder Foundation, 1986.

Bryson, John Moore. *Strategic Planning for Public and Nonprofit Organizations: A Guide to Strengthening and Sustaining Organizational Achievement.* San Francisco, CA: Jossey-Bass, 1988.

Burkhart, Patrick J. and Suzanne Reuss. *Successful Strategic Planning: A Guide for Nonprofit Agencies and Organizations.* Newbury Park, CA: Sage Pub., 1993.

Carver, John. *Boards That Make A Difference: A New Design for Leadership in Nonprofit and Public Organizations.* San Francisco, CA: Jossey-Bass Publishers, 1990.

Dolnick, Sandy F., (editor). *Fundraising for Nonprofit Institutions.* Greenwich, CT: JAI Press, 1987.

Espy, Siri N. *Handbook of Strategic Planning for Nonprofit Organizations.* New York, NY: Praeger, 1986.

Gelatt, James P. *Managing Nonprofit Organizations in the 21st Century.* Phoenix, AZ: Oryx Press, 1992.

Hardy, James M. *Managing for Impact in Nonprofit Organizations: Corporate Planning Techniques and Applications.* Erwin, TN: Essex Press, 1984.

Hay, Robert D. *Strategic Management in Non-Profit Organizations: An Administrator's Handbook.* New York: Quorum Books, 1990.

Howe, Fisher. *The Board Member's Guide to Fund Raising: What Every Trustee Needs to Know About Raising Money.* San Francisco, CA: Jossey Publishers, 1991.

Olenick, Arnold J. and Philip R. Olenick. *A Nonprofit Organization Operating Manual: Planning for Survival and Growth.* New York: Foundation Center, 1991.